PRAISE FOR

UNFLINCHING

National Bestseller

"*Unflinching* is one of those books that you just can't put down. What a book! What a life! Jody is an inspiration. He never quit, he never gave up, no matter how tough the road was. This book will make you proud that Jody is a Canadian."

—**DON CHERRY**

"A raw and sometimes brutal journey into the heart and life of a soldier."

—*Ottawa Magazine*

"I read it all, start to finish, in one enthralled session. *Unflinching* is raw, personal, unforgiving, unrelenting and draws one into Jody's life, with a vividness and a colour that's visceral."

—**GENERAL RICK HILLIER,** former Chief of
Defence Staff for the Canadian Forces

"The pacing and quiet drama of [Jody's] stories of battlefield missions are excellent. He's got a nice touch for keeping you glued to his narrative. And it's in his portrayal of the physical and psychological effects of intense combat and command tactical gaffes that the memoir really takes off."

—*Winnipeg Free Press*

"Pure Jody Mitic—smart, funny, honest and tough. I think the first time I saw Jody he was kicking the hell out of the army half marathon on his new feet; the next time, he was a newly elected Ottawa councillor; and now he's an accomplished storyteller. He'd be almost irritatingly capable if he wasn't also a lovely human being."

—**CHRISTIE BLATCHFORD,** author of *Fifteen Days:
Stories of Bravery, Friendship, Life and Death
from Inside the New Canadian Army*

"A frank and engaging biography, chronicling Mitic's transformation from troubled, awkward Brampton teen to self-assured infantryman."

—Edmonton Sun

"Jody Mitic's harrowing and heroic life story reveals Canada's front-line soldiers as I know them to be: intelligent, complex, emotional and loyal. . . . This book is inspiration for anyone hoping to re-invent their life. Jody has triumphed at it time and again."

—**KEVIN NEWMAN,** journalist/anchor and co-author of *All Out*

"Mitic's long and courageous road to recovery, from a life-changing injury and subsequent addiction to painkillers to becoming an outspoken advocate of injured veterans and an Ottawa city councillor, is the stuff of inspiring movies."

—Quill & Quire

"Over the last several years, Jody Mitic has been a larger-than-life figure in the military community. Reading his experiences in his own clear, humble, funny and no-bullshit prose has offered insight to the very real human at the core of his story. I would recommend *Unflinching* to any Canadian, military or civilian."

—**MATT LENNOX,** author of *The Carpenter* and *Knucklehead*

UNFLINCHING

THE MAKING OF A
CANADIAN
SNIPER

JODY MITIC
WITH PERRY LEFKO

PUBLISHED BY SIMON & SCHUSTER

NEW YORK LONDON TORONTO SYDNEY NEW DELHI

Simon & Schuster Canada
A Division of Simon & Schuster, Inc.
166 King Street East, Suite 300
Toronto, Ontario M5A 1J3

This Simon & Schuster Canada edition May 2016

SIMON & SCHUSTER CANADA and colophon are registered trademarks
of Simon & Schuster, Inc.

For information about special discounts for bulk purchases,
please contact Simon & Schuster Special Sales at 1-800-268-3216 or
CustomerService@simonandschuster.ca.

The author wishes to formally thank Perry Lefko for early development
of the project and believing in it as a modern-day Canadian war story.

Library and Archives Canada Cataloguing in Publication

Mitic, Jody, author
Unflinching : the making of a Canadian sniper / Jody Mitic.
Reprint. Originally published: 2015.
ISBN 978-1-4767-9511-9 (paperback)
1. Mitic, Jody. 2. Afghan War, 2001– —Personal narratives,
Canadian. 3. Canada. Canadian Armed Forces—
Biography. 4. Snipers—Canada—Biography. 5. Disabled veterans—
Canada—Biography. 6. City Council members—Ontario—
Ottawa—Biography. I. Title.
DS371.413.M58 2016   958.104'7371   C-2015-908126-2

Manufactured in the United States of America

3   5   7   9   10   8   6   4

All photographs in the insert are courtesy of the author,
except as marked.

*This book is dedicated to my fellow snipers
and to the men and women in the Canadian Armed Forces,
past, present and future.* Pro patria.

CONTENTS

Foreword by General Rick Hillier
xi

Prologue: Never Give Up
1

PART 1

1   The Soldier in the Child   *7*

2   Private Mitic   *15*

3   Unfit Soldier   *29*

4   Not Fit to Shoot a Dog   *47*

PART 2

5   For a Bit of Coloured Ribbon   *67*

6   The Patrolling Spirit   *73*

7   Lessons from Sniper School   *79*

8   The War on Terror Begins   *89*

9   Married to the Army   *97*

PART 3

10 Into Afghanistan: Improvise, Adapt, Overcome *109*

11 Operation Rocket Man *125*

12 Operation Medusa *139*

13 Hunter-Killer Sniper Team *163*

PART 4

14 Final Steps *193*

15 Cut Off *201*

16 Soldier On *213*

Epilogue: On My Own Two Feet
225

Acknowledgements
231

Jody's Glossary of Military Terms
235

FOREWORD

BY GENERAL RICK HILLIER, FORMER CHIEF OF
DEFENCE STAFF FOR THE CANADIAN FORCES

Perpetual optimism is a force multiplier. It costs nothing to give, is priceless and has the power to transform people instantly. Jody Mitic is a shining example of how perpetual optimism works, of how one person's resolute determination spreads hope far and wide—because if he could pick himself up and begin anew after becoming a casualty of war, there's hope for all of us as we face life's challenges. A friend of mine who loved being a soldier used to say, "If this doesn't light your fire, your wood's all wet." This attitude epitomizes Jody—a soldier's soldier—just as accurately.

I read *Unflinching*, start to finish, in one enthralled session. It is a raw, personal, unforgiving and unrelenting portrait of life as a soldier, told with a vividness and colour that is visceral. It will take you through Jody's early days in the military, where he began the way we all did—as a young soldier learning the ropes, honing self-discipline and stamina, qualities that would later serve him well on his various tours of duty in Afghanistan and elsewhere. This book is an insider's look at the training involved to become an elite sniper and the particular acuity this role entails. But more than anything, it offers a kind of travel opportunity, allowing the reader to walk a mile in Jody's army boots, and, later, to run alongside him in his prosthetics as he races—often literally—towards a new and bright future.

UNFLINCHING

PROLOGUE

NEVER GIVE UP

IT WAS 2007. I was a master corporal and sniper team leader in the Canadian Armed Forces. I'd just celebrated my thirtieth birthday in Afghanistan. I'd survived three tours over the course of seven years. I had been preparing for war for my entire adult life. But nothing prepared me for what was about to happen next.

On January 11, a week after my birthday, our three-man elite sniper unit—Barry, Kash and me—led by my boss, Gord, was sent on a mission. We were to intercept Taliban insurgents fleeing the Canadian Forces as we advanced on an Afghan village. We stepped through the wire at Strong Point Centre and headed through the thick mud of a farmer's field. A while later, we arrived at an opening in a wall leading into the village. I was bringing up the rear and I couldn't see what was ahead, but Barry could. Barry was my point man and was always razor-sharp.

Two small steps led up to the low entry. Two small steps.

Barry went through the opening first, followed by Gord and Kash, rifles at the ready. They all cleared the entry without issue. I was up next.

I took those two steps up, clearing the entry. In the green glow of my night vision, I saw Kash covering the six o'clock position. I tapped him on the shoulder to signal that I was in position and he moved to follows the others. We always keep ten metres between us when we are moving, just in case something goes wrong.

I sensed Kash moving away from me as I watched our rear for threats. When I felt the right amount of time had passed, I looked over my shoulder to confirm we were keeping the proper spacing. I took one last look at our rear and then turned to follow the team. But as my right foot touched the ground, a massive orange fireball soared across my face. For a few seconds I was floating, weightless, suspended in space and time. I didn't hear a sound.

The next thing I knew, I was on the ground. My mouth, eyes, ears and nose were full of dirt. I was confused. My night vision was gone. Where was my trusty C-8 carbine? I'd had it at my side for the last five months. And then the pain hit—a pain so intense that it completely overwhelmed my body.

Such a small thing, an anti-personnel land mine—about the size and shape of a thick hockey puck—but full of deadly explosives.

I am not very religious, but they say there are no atheists in fox-holes. As I punched the ground as hard as I could, I screamed, "Oh god! Oh god! Oh god!"

My fellow snipers rushed to my side. "Sorry, guys. I just fucked the mission." At that moment, this was all I cared about.

"Fuck, Jody. Don't worry about it, man," Barry said. It was dark. My eyes were full of mud. I tried to look down at my legs but I couldn't. Barry crouched over me, blocking my view. Whatever was going on with my legs, he didn't want me to see it.

The next hour was the longest of my life. Your mind goes to the weirdest places in a situation like that. I was so thirsty but refused to drink much. I remembered an episode of M*A*S*H in which

Hawkeye says it's a bad idea for the severely wounded to chug water. For some reason, in that moment, I chose to take medical advice from a TV show that had been off the air for decades.

With each passing minute, I was growing weaker and weaker. Barry and Gord were both kneeling next to me doing first aid as Kash kept watch for signs of the enemy.

"Do you think I'm going to make it?" I asked.

"Of course you're going to make it. Never give up, Jody. You know that."

Never. Give. Up. The phrase repeated over and over in my head. It still does to this day.

Dear Dad,   July 17, 1994
   This is starting to get bad. They
make us do stuff that sucks. Last
night they had us working until
9:00. We usually get off at 6:30
7:00. So I was up until around
12:00 doing laundry. This sucks. I'm
tired, I'm sore, real sore. Now the
NCO's think they are real cool by
making us double time every where
we go. After breakfast, lunch and
supper. People are puking every where,
my whole right leg and hip are fucked.
I don't know how much longer I can
keep this shit up. Now they're talking
about canceling our next day off AND
not letting us off base for the rest of
the course. I just shot the machine
gun. It was okay. I'm confused though.
I get more of a kick out of shooting
my C-7 rifle, then I get out of
shooting rocket launchers or machine guns.
all well screw it.
   Well it's 11:00 pm. I would like to be in bed
but hey. I've got to do laundry. Here's a
list of what you could mail me.
1. 8-12 pair 100% cotton socks.
2. 6-8 pair 100% wool(grey) socks.
3. 4-5 pair boxer underwear.
4. Tapes- Beatie Boys, U2 Zooropa, Big Sugar (both),
        Crow soundtrack, Nine Inch Nails,
5. Comics- Anything on my pile. Just buy me a
        dozen.
6. GOODIES-Anything you can think of plus
        chocolate chip cookies.
7. Bug coils- Maybe.
   Thanks. Tell Cory to get the tapes
and comics. Put my check in the bank.
                    LOVE JODY.

PART 1

Out of every one hundred men, ten shouldn't even be there, eighty are just targets, nine are the real fighters, and we are lucky to have them, for they make the battle. Ah, but the one, one is a warrior, and he will bring the others back.

—HERACLITUS

1

THE SOLDIER IN THE CHILD

M Y MOM was never keen to let me play with guns when I was a kid—which is not the way you would expect a story about a Canadian sniper to start. She was irate when somebody gave me a cap-gun rifle for my seventh birthday.

"What do they think they're doing, giving a kid a weapon? No son of mine is going to shoot his way out of situations."

"But, Mom, I'm not going to shoot at *people*. I'm going to shoot at *stuff*."

"Stuff? Stuff like what?"

"Um, cans?"

My mother sighed. "You can stand on the front porch—and only on the front porch—and you can play with the rifle there, shooting at 'stuff' . . . or cans. Only that. Got it?"

"Sure, Mom." It was hard to hide my glee. From that moment on, I practised shooting all the time. I loved that little gun. I'd load it with a roll of caps, which had eight shots in each one, and I'd aim at just about anything, pretending the gun was real. I vividly remember the

JODY MITIC

sound it made, that distinct *Pop!*, and the smoke that used to come
out after each little explosion. It didn't take me long to use up all
the caps. Then Mom refused to buy me more. But that didn't stop
me from running around with the gun and hearing the sound in my
head.

When I wasn't on the porch, I would often pretend to shoot with
a hockey stick that I imagined into a gun. When I asked Mom for
some G.I. Joe action figures, the response was clear: "No." But I didn't
give up asking, and eventually she relented, under one condition:
"Jody, none of your G.I. Joes can be carrying weapons." My shoulders
slumped. If they weren't carrying weapons, what was the point?

Beyond just playing with guns, one of my favourite games was War.
At Grandma and Grandpa's house, I'd watch World War II documen-
taries, and then I'd re-enact war scenes in their basement with my
cousins. There was a stockpile of past Christmas gifts at Grandma and
Grandpa's—including plastic guns and rifles that fired suction darts—
and all of us kids would go wild down in that basement. The two
couches at either end became our fortresses, and we'd throw pillows
at each other simulating bombs and grenades. We got so into it that
every single one of us kids shed blood at one point or another, usually
when the pillows were put aside and we started throwing "grenades"
that were a little heavier. We all have scars from when things got a
little out of hand.

Even when I was very young, I'd always choose to play the role of
the sniper. Some of the other kids would want to be commanders or
tank drivers or pilots, but not me. If there was a toy weapon with a
scope on it, I would choose it. I'd pretend to aim, taking my time to
actually imagine where the bullet would hit, then I'd imaginary-shoot
at one of my "enemy" cousins.

I guess you could blame my fascination with guns and the military
on my uncle Jim, who was in the Canadian Armed Forces. When I

was a little kid, I remember waiting for Uncle Jim to arrive for the holidays. The doorbell would ring and I'd go running to the door. We'd open up, and there Uncle Jim would be—in full uniform, robust, with sandy-brown hair and his signature moustache—holding out a teddy bear for me. When I was a kid, I thought Uncle Jim was the coolest guy ever. He'd tell stories from his time in the army, and even though I didn't always understand everything, I understood enough to know that Uncle Jim was a bit of a badass, and to me, that was amazing. His presence had a profound and positive impact on my impressionable young mind. As I grew older, Uncle Jim always fed my interest in his line of work.

When I was about twelve, Uncle Jim took me on a private tour of the Canadian Forces Borden air base, north of Toronto. I stood next to real-life fighter jets, not LEGO replicas I'd built in my bedroom. I distinctly remember feeling so small beside those planes, and yet feeling secure in my awe of that type of firepower.

When I was a bit older, *Top Gun* came out in theatres, and my dreams of becoming an F-14 pilot were born. It was a short-lived dream.

"Uncle Jim," I said, "I want to be like Tom Cruise! I want to fly an F-14!"

Uncle Jim broke it to me in his dry, matter-of-fact tone, the one he reserved for times like this. "Jody, the Canadian Armed Forces doesn't have F-14s. We don't have aircraft carriers. We don't have a Top Gun school. We have about three hundred pilots in the force, with only a hundred F-18s."

Okay then, I thought. I was too good-looking to fly planes anyway. Back to the original dream of being a "ground pounder" in the good ol' infantry.

So that was Mom and Uncle Jim. Then there was my dad.

Dad wasn't as opposed to my military fascination as my mom was.

He'd grown up poor, and to him, guns were a regular part of life. They were used for hunting and for bringing home extra food for the family. When I was a kid, Dad showed me the shotguns he'd used when he was younger to shoot at rabbits—single- and double-barrelled guns. He told me about my uncle Pete, his younger brother, who apparently was an amazing shot. According to family lore, Uncle Pete once saw a rabbit go bounding over a fence and was so quick with the shotgun that he killed it in midair.

When I was little, Dad used to say, "When you're old enough, Jody, you and me are going to go hunting, just like I did when I was a boy." But life had changed so much since he was a kid, and as I got older, Dad had to devote a lot of his time and energy to his job. He didn't have time for some of his dreams, which by that point had also become my dreams. He was a middle-class workingman doing his best to look after his family—including me; my younger brother, Cory; and my little sister, Katie.

When I was five, we moved from Kitchener, Ontario, to Winnipeg because my dad was hired on to the staff at the Canadian Auto Workers union. We were all excited for him and proud. But this change in my dad's job was the root of troubles between him and Mom. I had a great childhood overall, but because of Dad's work, he was rarely home, and that was tough on Mom. When I was ten, Dad shot to the top of the organization, becoming one of four assistant vice-presidents to "Uncle Buzz," as we knew him—Buzz Hargrove to everyone else. We moved from Winnipeg to Brampton as part of Dad's promotion. I remember the sounds of that house—the slamming of the front door, and even the sound of shattering glass when that door was slammed too hard one day after an argument between Mom and Dad.

My parents eventually split up when I was a teenager. This wasn't a huge shock to me, but for Cory, who's almost five years younger than me, and for Katie, who's six years my junior, it was probably harder to process. My dad bought a condo across town in Brampton and still lives there. Cory, Katie and I lived with Mom in a house in Brampton.

Mom was the decision maker on the home front. She was the commanding officer and the sergeant major. As commanding officer, she'd give us our orders: "I want those bedrooms cleaned, now." Then she'd return a while later in her role as Sergeant Major to inspect our work and make sure we'd done it right. And even though she stood only about five foot four, she was tough and anything but a pushover.

"Mom, I want to play the drums. I want to rock and roll!"

"No. Too loud. Too expensive. Play the piano. Everyone plays the piano."

"Mom, I want to take tae kwon do and do other martial arts. Bruce Lee kicks! Hee-ya!"

Crickets.

Even though she didn't always support my whims, Mom did an amazing job of raising three kids. This was a woman who'd lost her own parents to a car accident when she was only ten years old. She and her siblings ended up scattered and she lived in a foster home for a good chunk of her childhood. Did she ever get the support she needed? I somehow doubt it. But one thing was clear: she would do anything for her kids, and she was fierce. I was a big reader when I was young, and still am. I'd read anything, from newspapers to comics to *The Lord of the Rings*. I got that trait from Mom, who read at every chance she got.

"Mom, what are you reading?"

"A book about parenting."

"Why?"

"So I can do a good job of raising you. You think this is easy?"

Even then, I knew it wasn't. Mom had to learn on the go. I give her a ton of credit for being an amazing mother, even at the most difficult times, and in my teenage years, I made sure there were plenty of those.

I was a tall and gangly teen. There are pictures of me when I was fourteen and my legs look so disproportionate to the rest of me. I was about six foot one, weighed only about 135 pounds and had bad acne. I wasn't exactly popular on the high school scene. And after we moved from Winnipeg, I had a hard time adjusting to the school system in Ontario. I was a loner who didn't fit in. I still dreamt of being in the army, probably because I wanted to belong to something, and it was definitely clear I didn't belong in school.

When I was fourteen, I had the usual teenage depression, but I probably took things too far when I decided to run away from home. I had started hanging around with some kids who had been in a group home. They seemed way more interesting than the regular kids at high school, and I tried to do what they did, including taking up smoking. Funny that at the time, these kids meant the world to me—they made me feel that I finally belonged to something, a group where I fit in and had a role to play—but I can't remember a single one of their names today.

On the day I took off, I wrote a note to my parents saying I didn't want to live at home anymore and that I was leaving for good. I took the keys to my mom's car and headed out with a bunch of these kids from the group home. I had never been behind the wheel of a car before. But I had always paid close attention to Dad when he drove, and I figured it out.

We put some camping gear in the trunk and I withdrew all the money I had in my bank account—about $200. We were going to drive all the way to Mexico. Oh yeah. We had it *all* figured out. The whole experience lasted about four days. We didn't have a map or a real plan or even ID, and we were getting very close to the U.S. border. All of my money had gone up in smoke by that point—literally, in the form of cigarettes. A couple of the kids had already bailed on our trip and had gone back to the group home. One of the other guys said he could get some cash from his sister in Mississauga, so we drove all the way back to the Greater Toronto Area. While he was in the apartment getting the money, I was startled by a knock on the window. A police officer was staring down at me. I rolled down the window.

"Driver's licence?"

"Um. I don't have one," I said.

He walked back to his cruiser, hopped in and stayed there for a few minutes. When he returned, he leaned into the driver's-side window and said, "Okay, Jody. So why did you run away from home?"

I didn't give him any answers because I didn't have any.

"You best come with me, then," he said, and led me to his cruiser. Once there, I heard the general alert go out on the radio with my name and description. The officer grabbed his radio.

"I've got him in the back of my car." The officer looked at me in the rearview mirror. "He's safe and sound."

My dad picked me up at the police station. We were both totally silent for most of the drive back home. Neither of us knew what to say. Then Dad reached out to me and pulled me to him. He said, "Jody, son, I don't know what's going on with you, but I'm just glad you're home." I broke down and said how sorry I was and that I was glad to be home and so glad to see him, too.

When I walked through the front door, Mom was there. She immediately gave me a big hug, but we didn't talk much at that point because my brother and sister were there. They, too, just looked on quietly, confused by everything that was happening.

I think this was a massive wake-up call for our family. Children's Aid wanted my parents to lay criminal charges against me for grand theft auto and also charge the kids I was with, but my parents had no intention of pursing anything along those lines. They understood, even if I had trouble saying what it was, that I was acting out because something was wrong. Looking back now, I can see that I felt like such a misfit that I wanted to disappear. It was only later, once I was in the army, that I realized how much a sense of belonging had been missing when I was younger.

I kept a journal at this time, full of the usual adolescent angst. "No one understands me!" or so I thought. "None of you cares!" or so I thought. The fact that my parents arranged for me to see a psychologist didn't factor into "care" in my mind. But that connection helped me a lot. I started thinking more deeply about what I wanted to do with my life. Did I really want to just escape everything and run away? Did I want to keep hanging around with nice but aimless kids from a group home? Did I have any talents at all? Any interests I wanted to pursue? Did I want to keep upsetting my mom and dad? Finally, did I want to make something, anything, of my life?

And that's when I made a big decision for myself, one that was finally a step in the right direction, one that was the first step down a path that would lead me to a military career.

"I want to join the army, the militia. It won't interfere with school, Mom. During the week I'll be a student, and on the weekends I'll be a soldier, a Weekend Warrior . . . but I need your consent."

"Well, we all knew this day was coming," my mother said.

I put a pen and the consent form into my mom's hands. She signed the form.

The next hurdle was getting my high school transcript to hand in with the form. I had to borrow a loonie from my girlfriend to do so. "Really?" she said, handing me the coin. "I can't believe I'm helping you get yourself killed."

I laughed. "This is Canada," I said. "When was the last time we went to war?"

And that's how it all started.

2

PRIVATE MITIC

I BECAME A member of the Lorne Scots regiment of the militia in Brampton, Ontario, on May 1, 1994. I was seventeen years old and I'd just spent three years in high school. School to me felt like an obstacle to the only two things I was interested in—getting in the army or becoming a cop. My teachers didn't seem to understand me, and except for a few, they had nothing to offer me.

I joined the Lorne Scots hoping to find something I was missing. Enrolled in the reserves, I was volunteering to live part of my life as a soldier and the rest as a civilian. If ever there was a threat and Canada needed soldiers, the militia would be called on for active duty.

Before joining, I had long hair like Mel Gibson's character in *Lethal Weapon 2*. I went to the barber with a photo of a U.S. Marine in hand.

"Make me look like this," I said, showing him a photo of the high-and-tight Marine jarhead cut I wanted.

The barber nodded. "You're the customer," he said, grabbed his clippers and gave me my very first army-style cut. Militia guys worked or went to school. They lived as civilians most of the time and trained as soldiers only once a week and on weekends, so they didn't usually keep their hair army-short.

Once the barber was done, I studied myself in his mirror. I barely recognized the young man staring back at me. The eyes were the same, but everything else was different. I wasn't Jody Mitic, layabout loner, high school good-for-nothing, another floundering adolescent with no ambition and no life plan. That kid was lying under a pile of hair on the floor. Looking back at me was Jody Mitic, soldier in training.

My friends teased me about my new look and so did the guys in the militia. My family was blown away. I remember coming home from the swearing-in ceremony in uniform. Once we walked through the door, Mom said, "Jody, I'm so proud of you." I didn't know what to say. She continued: "You stuck by your goal, Jody. You went after this. You went to the recruitment office for information, you gathered all the right paperwork. Then you filled out all the forms and delivered them. You convinced me and your dad that this was the right thing for you, even when we had our doubts. You never gave up on what you wanted. You never quit. And look at you now." Making Mom proud felt really good. Even though I never said it at the time, that was an important moment for me.

A few weeks later, school was out, and I took a Greyhound bus from Brampton right to the Canadian Forces base at Petawawa, Ontario, where I would spend the summer. On that bus were a whole bunch of young kids who looked just like me, but also older guys who'd decided to sign up. We stepped off the bus and suddenly we were in a totally foreign landscape. We were completely stunned. Tents were set up around the area, but there wasn't much else besides a few dirt roads.

As recruits, we had no idea what we'd just stepped into.

"What now?" a kid next to me said under his breath.

"Fuck if I know," I answered.

"Why the fuck are you all standing around!" We turned around and saw some hard-looking non-commissioned officers—or NCOs—who minutes earlier hadn't been paying us any mind. Now they turned into demons as they walked our way. "There's work to do! See this truck? It's got your barrack boxes and kit bags on it. I want everything off that truck in five minutes. Let's GO!"

We had arrived that morning as high school kids going to what we thought of as summer camp. Within moments, we were deep into the shit. The next four hours were a whirlwind of organized chaos, with everyone being yelled at, fingers being pointed and equipment being thrown around. Deficiencies were pointed out that had not been deficiencies five minutes earlier. Some kids were crying. Two or three instructors would gang up on one kid in the group and give him or her hell. So much for the Welcome Wagon! I remember thinking to myself, "What have I gotten myself into?" I was just a wide-eyed teen with no idea about the inner workings of the Armed Forces except for what I'd learned from my uncle and from movies.

Once all the dust had settled and everyone seemed to have yelled themselves out, the instructors broke us into groups and platoons. We got a basic introduction to military rank structure and organizational format before being ordered to our bunk space in the barracks. We were actually living in a tent, but as we learned then, whether a soldier is on the ground in a tent or in a high-rise condo, that space is his or her barracks, and it must be kept clean and organized.

Before we went to bed, we were given a talking to by a large, red-headed sergeant with a thick moustache. To us, he looked like a veteran of a hundred wars. "Each section will have a master corporal who's in charge and a corporal who's 2IC—second in command. There are four sections to this platoon and four platoons to this company. I am your platoon warrant officer, and this"—he pointed to a lean, iron-hard man with a stern look and (of course) a moustache—"is your platoon commander. You will sweep your barracks every day.

You will keep your kit clean and dry. You will learn the rank structure and address everybody by rank. You will know your place, and it is at the bottom. Understood?"

"Yes, sir!" Loud and clear. Pond scum we were until we proved otherwise, until we earned our right to be soldiers.

We were a fairly diverse group in the militia that summer—mostly white guys like me, but also some Indians, Asians and blacks. And there were several young women in our platoons, too, in the same tents alongside the men. This was shortly after the Canadian government allowed women to perform military combat roles on the front.

"There will be no separation between males and females in platoons. Deal with it," we were told. So we did. After a couple of weeks, I didn't even notice when a girl was changing in front of me. None of us had the energy or the time to notice each other anyway. The only difference between girls and the rest of us was that some of them had long hair, which they had to wear in a single braid. As guys, if our hair ever grew past the tops of our ears, we were reamed out pretty fast. We were expected to stay clean-shaven, too, which for a kid with bad acne was not my favourite rule. But I quickly learned that my personal preferences meant nothing here.

Not only was our hair inspected and our uniforms and our barracks, but also our feet, underarms and crotches. Medics came by every couple of days looking for signs of rashes and fungus. Medics in the army are kind of like your mommy, and that's true even if they happen to be men. They are the ones who make sure you're physically well and hold you accountable if you don't take care of yourself. Small injuries can become big injuries in a hurry, and medics make sure soldiers consider their physical well-being. Later, when I became a combat soldier, I saw just how important medics were. In the infantry, we are trained to be tough, and because of that we often ignore or downplay injuries, which can lead to problems later. Without that objective third-person review, small things can turn a soldier into a casualty, and I saw that for the first time with monkey bum in the militia.

"Make sure you powder your ass and balls, troops! Ladies, you do the same with your bits. We are going for a long march and you don't want to get monkey bum."

"What the hell is that?" I asked.

The master corporal smiled. He was about to instill some "veteran's wisdom." "If you neglect your personal hygiene and ignore my instructions to powder yourselves, you will get chafed from all the drills and from running in wet gear. You will get a rash. And you will start walking like a monkey because your ass crack is itching so bad. There you have it, troops. Monkey bum." I immediately pulled out my foot powder and dumped a generous amount into the front and back of my underwear before we set out on the day's march. I got monkey bum anyway. And of course, the medic noticed. He let me suffer for the day before silently handing me some Penaten baby cream. What a relief!

There was a system for everything in the army, a way to stand and a way to sit, a way to dress and a way to sleep. There was also a system for how to properly eat at the mess hall. We would line up for food with a plate, cup and KFS—knife, fork and spoon—and the cooks would dish out the food onto our plates. It was pretty basic but overall good food, considering these guys were literally feeding an army— meat and potatoes, some milk and maybe a cookie for dessert. One thing you learn quickly is never to piss off the army cook or the army clerk. The clerk pays you and the cook feeds you. As Napoleon said, "An army marches on its stomach."

At the mess hall, one master corporal in particular watched over us like a hawk. He seemed to enjoy making everything as difficult as possible, especially mealtimes. As soon as we were in formation awaiting dismissal so we could go eat, he would stand there staring at his watch, his bushy moustache twitching, "You . . . people . . . have

. . . eight . . . minutes . . . to . . . eat!" He yelled just like that, with giant pauses between each word and pivoting higher and higher on his tippy toes with each word. We would run around like headless chickens, trying to get our food, find a place to sit and eat our meals within this eight-minute deadline.

All the while, he'd be barking at us, "You better hurry up and get your fucking food! Don't miss your timings! Miss your timing and people die!"

Once, early in the summer, we stopped to eat in a field while we were learning to navigate. We were served a "hay box" meal from a truck. I got my food, found a spot to sit and put my plate down. I jumped up to grab something from the food line, and when I ran back to my spot, my plate was covered in baby grasshoppers.

"What the fuck is this?" I said under my breath. The guys around me shrugged. I flicked the insects off my plate and out of my cup of soup. Then I ate the food anyhow. This is what happened to those who left their plates unattended. But within a few weeks of arriving, we were so tired that when grasshoppers jumped into our gravy and mashed potatoes, we didn't bother picking them out. We just ate them.

Meanwhile, our instructors revelled in the show. Every once in a while, I'd catch the satisfied smirk of our officers and some of our NCOs as they watched us eat bugs without even flinching. No one was being mean or sadistic to us; this was just part of training, and we were toughening up well. We were learning to be soldiers.

Sleeping arrangements were about as deluxe as the food. We slept in sleeping bags on top of canvas folding cots with wooden shipping pallets underneath them. And it's not like we had pillows to make our beds softer. Tough was the lesson, and we toughed it out, day and night.

Our routine was an endless, monotonous cycle. We woke up. We made up our cots, folding our sleeping bags in the exact way we'd been taught. We swept off our shipping pallets. Even the shipping pallets had to be treated like priceless equipment, wiped off every day so they were free of mud. The guy who decided to let that slide was in for an earful from the inspecting NCO.

Once the tent was in shape, it was on to barrack boxes. We had to lay them out as instructed, with everything in its proper place, whether that made sense or not. We had to stand beside our kit and cots, everyone perfectly still as the officer did inspection. At the time, I thought that so much of this discipline was overkill. Why did we have to stand at attention when the officer was on the other side of the tent looking at some other dude's cot and kit? Why did our barrack boxes have to be identical? It took me a couple years to figure out that the skills they were drilling into us then are actually really important for a combat leader. If you can't stand still long enough for morning inspection, how can your commanders trust you to hold your post during a mortar barrage? How will a leader know he can count on you to be a useful soldier if you can't even follow through on an order meant to keep you and your comrades safe, even if you don't know it at the time? All these drills were training me to put self-discipline above my instinct to flee or flinch. When everything in me told me to break my posture, to stand down, I learned to obey a different order instead. It was basic training, but I was assimilating some important skills that later would make me a better sniper.

Beyond keeping order in our tents and in the mess hall, those first few weeks were spent on other basic military skills—marching and parading, saluting, identifying enemy (as in Russian) aircraft and ve-hicles . . . and rifle drill.

"These are your weapons," the master corporal told us, giving out our rifles. Finally I was holding an actual rifle. I couldn't quite be-lieve it. It was awesome, the coolest thing ever. Because I didn't know any better at the time, this simple rifle looked like an M16 I'd seen in movies about Vietnam. It was actually a C7, the Canadian Forces' standard issue, with a carrying handle on top, composite foreguards and a solid rifle butt. I'd only ever seen guns like this one on TV, and here I was holding one in my hands.

The master corporal began his lesson. "First," he said, "this isn't a gun, it's a rifle. And you should know that this rifle can be used for all sorts of things beyond just shooting. It's exactly one metre long, which means you can use it to measure both objects and distances." He went on to explain that when we built fighting trenches, which had to be three metres by one metre, we were to measure the correct dimensions using our rifles. "You are going to learn how to use this rifle, and you will use it how we tell you to. And as I said, it's not just about shooting. First, you need to learn how to care for your weapon, how to keep it clean, how to store it, how to carry it, and how not to do something stupid with it that could hurt yourself or one of your fellow soldiers. After you get all of that, you might be lucky enough to learn how to shoot it. Got it?"

The master corporal demonstrated how to lay a rifle down in the right position. Then he walked the line. When he came to me, he paused.

"What are you, a fucking *individual*?" he said, flipping my rifle onto the other side.

"Sorry, I—"

"Don't apologize! Just do things right the first time." He explained why we always lay the rifle on its right side to prevent dirt from getting into the ejector slot, which can jam your gun.

"Got it? Watch. And learn, recruit."

The word "individual" is one of the biggest insults you can have thrown at you in the military world. The military runs on teamwork. Individuals can't be counted on.

We were taught the basic principles of marksmanship—like how to position and hold the rifle firmly, how to naturally align it with the target without physical effort, and how to release and follow through without disturbance of position. I picked a spot. I grounded myself the way I'd been told to. I aimed. I fired. And I learned that I was a natural shooter.

We also learned how to zero our rifles. Every rifle has sights that need to be carefully adjusted to fit the shooter. To zero a rifle, you line up on the target and shoot five times. Then you check where the bullets hit compared with where you were aiming. If you're four inches left and low, you've got to compensate four inches right and high. To do this, you adjust the front and back sights and try again, until you meet the target. Once you've done that, your weapon is yours and yours alone. Sure, you can pick up any rifle and hit a target roughly from a hundred metres, but to shoot from longer distances with any accuracy, you're going to need your own zeroed rifle.

I remember after we finished shooting for the first time, I stood at ease, putting the rifle butt next to my right baby toe and holding it by the front sight, called the iron sight. It's a steel attachment fitted to the barrel. As well as being used to aim, it helps dissipate the heat of the bullet, which I discovered the second it touched the web of my hand so soon after firing. The sight was very hot, and I flinched when I touched it, but I didn't yell or say anything. Out of the corner of my eye, I noticed a few other guys pulling away and shaking their hands at the burn. This was a typical rite of passage. Some of our instructors looked on, smiling, while others shook their heads at the guys who made a big deal out of it.

"Your rifle is a dangerous weapon. Don't get burned. Lesson learned, recruits."

There were some things they wanted us to figure out on our own, and our resolve was being tested and watched even then.

Soon enough, we learned to shoot at different ranges and targets. At the firing range, we practised a drill where we'd all be lined up in lanes. The range was 500 metres long, and every hundred metres, there'd be a mound where you would shoot from. We started at the

400 metre mound in a prone position on the ground. Range safety officers behind us kept us all moving at the same pace, more or less shoulder to shoulder, about five metres apart, for safety reasons. We were told to load, ready our rifles, then put the safety on. A target would pop up ahead and we'd have about forty-five seconds to run forward, catch our breath and shoot the target ten times. But you can't just aim and shoot. You had to breathe in, hold it and then shoot. And you'd be doing this in the heat, while running. And let's not forget that besides your rifle you had your helmet, your ammo and webbing and your water. By the time I made it to the 100 metre mound, my heart was racing. I could see I was hitting the target, because the wood splinters from the two-by-four it was nailed to were exploding out the back, which was always a good feeling. I loved those drills. It felt incredible. I had my own rifle, and I was shooting it in simulated combat situations.

Once we had learned to shoot our rifles, we moved on to pepper-potting. Why on earth it's called that, I don't know, but pepper-potting is the basic building block for movement in combat. Out in an open field in Petawawa, we practised a frontal attack on the enemy force, Cold War style.

"This is the way it works," we were told. "First, I explain. Then, I demonstrate. Then, you guys do." The master corporal and corporal showed us the technique of "up, he sees me, down." It was fast, it was violent, it was aggressive. I was pumped.

In our pairs, one guy would move forward while the other guy would shoot to provide cover. The mover would yell "Moving!" and jump up and move forward about three steps, saying "up, he sees me, down" in his head while his partner covered him. At "down," the mover would take cover going to ground, taking up a firing position and yelling "Covering!" once in position. Then his partner would move forward in the same way. The idea was to always have a foot on the ground, which means one soldier is covering while the other is moving.

It was time for my fire-team partner and me to give the technique a try. Off I went, jumping up and seeing the "enemy" (really a bush we had picked a hundred metres away). So far, so good. But when I dropped to the ground, I was in such a hurry trying to be aggressive that my momentum was too strong and I slammed into the ground so hard that I knocked the wind out of myself. I hit the bottom of my chin off my rifle butt. I was stunned. It felt as though I'd just been punched. My vision narrowed and my ears were ringing, faintly at first but then more loudly. I heard, "Mitic! Mitic, get fucking moving! On your feet! Speed and aggression!" I sprang up, more on instinct than anything else, and stumbled on to gloriously destroy the imaginary enemy next to the bush.

I eventually came to my senses, but later that day, when it was time to practise again, I dropped down and landed on a blank round casing with a crimped end. It felt like a nail had been hammered through my kneecap, but I kept moving. To this day, I still have a star-shaped scar. That was my first experience advancing to contact with the "enemy."

All of this practice was a buildup to the PWT, or personal weapons test. We needed to pass that test to become infantry soldiers. It was the same drill that we'd done on the range, where we'd have to shoot from the mounds at targets that popped up, move forward to the next mound and shoot again. But this time, all our hits and misses would be calculated for a total score. Hit enough, pass. Miss too many, game over. I did the test just the way I had during the practice, hoping for the best.

Once it was over, our platoon warrant sat us down. "Okay, troops. You've all passed your PWT, so fuck you." That was good to hear, because I sure didn't want to have to do it again.

"Oh, and Mitic, you're the best shot. Congratu-fuckin'-lations."

"What?" I said.

"Yeah, you got the highest score, so . . . whatever. Good for you."
There wasn't a trophy or any fanfare, but I was pretty happy with this
outcome. I had no idea I'd done that well. This was the first real ac-
colade I received in the military world.

•

By the end of summer, I wasn't an aimless teen anymore. I was strong
and fit. I was orderly and organized. I could shoot a rifle. I could run
with equipment on. I could camouflage myself in the woods. I could
keep myself and my pack dry, even in damp conditions, which doesn't
sound like much, but it's an essential combat skill. At the end of it all,
I felt like a soldier.

I was one of the youngest guys there, not just in our platoon but in
the four platoons that made up our company. I still had another year
left of high school, but I wanted to join the regular Canadian Armed
Forces right then and there. My parents had other ideas.

"Look, Jody," my dad said. "There's nothing stopping you from
joining the army after high school, but why not stay in school now
and see that through? If you still feel the same once you graduate,
then fine. You can enlist then."

I must say that the summer in Petawawa had a profound effect
on my attitude in all kinds of ways. First, I was actually listening to
what my parents had to say, something I hadn't always done previous
to that. Second, when I took their advice and went back to school in
September, I was much more comfortable in the classroom.

Before militia training, I'd been so bored at school and found everything tedious and pointless. But after eight weeks of soldier training, school seemed like a breeze. I started arriving on time and paying
attention to lessons. In the military, you can direct your career according to your aptitudes and interests, so I decided to do the same

at school. Instead of taking classes I hated, I picked ones I knew I would enjoy. My grades improved because I was doing more of what I wanted to do. For the first time, I had discipline and self-direction, and instead of all that energy being repressed or coming out in the wrong way, I had focus.

I went from being a loner and keeping to myself to becoming more outgoing and popular at school. It helped that I was one of the few kids in high school who had wheels—my dad had bought me an '86 Dodge Ram pickup truck with the legendary slant six engine and the ram's-head hood emblem. I loved that truck.

By the time March break rolled around, I was eager to get back to military training. Our regiment flew down to Florida to participate in Southern Strike, a training session held at a U.S. National Guard base. Canadian regular forces—full-time military—trained with us, and it was one of the first times I worked with full-time soldiers. I got to ride in a C-130 Hercules military plane for the first time in some simulated combat exercises. The pilot took off with full power, pointing the nose straight up and doing circles high in the air while changing altitude every few seconds. I'd always had problems with amusement park rides that would spin you around, and this felt like that, except about ten times worse. I thought I was going to puke inside my helmet, but luckily I managed to keep my lunch down.

The week passed and it was back to school. I spent the next few months with renewed energy and focus. When the school year ended, I passed all my courses and got decent grades, a fact that both pleased and surprised my parents. It felt good to not be a source of concern to them as I had been in the past, and I knew they were proud of me now that my life was coming together. Of course, that didn't mean I had carte blanche to join the military. They still had their reservations. That summer, my dad came up with a plan.

"Son, why don't you work on the assembly line at the Lear auto parts plant in Oakville? It's a great job, with great pay—eight hundred dollars a week."

Eight hundred a week? For a teenager? It was hard to say no to that. Add to it that I was dating a girl who was still in high school. I could delay enlisting for a little while longer. And who knows, maybe my dad was right. Maybe I'd like working at a factory and making good money and buying cool things. Maybe that would be enough. Maybe that would be my life.

But as the year lingered on, I was dying a little bit inside every day. I hated working at the plant, the monotony of it, the lack of challenge. Sure, I had a cool car, cellphone and a ton of spending money and a great girlfriend, but something was missing.

The more I worked, the less time I devoted to the militia. And the less time I devoted to the militia, the more my ambition waned. My weekends were spent vegetating on the couch, when I wasn't wasting time and brain cells at night clubs. I was slipping into an old pattern of restlessness and I didn't like it. I needed to make a decision: was I going to be an assembly-line worker for the rest of my life or was I going to pursue my dream of being a real soldier?

One day, during a coffee break at the plant, I called the clerk at my unit, the Lorne Scots.

"I'm ready," I said.

"For what?" she asked.

"I'm ready to make a career of this. I'm ready to put in my application to the regular forces."

And with that, I went from earning $800 a week to $500 every two weeks. In 1997, the Armed Forces were still in the "decade of darkness," which meant pay rates were frozen and Force Reduction Program (FRP) was in full effect. Just as the Canadian military was being downsized and senior soldiers were being offered buyouts, I was opting in. The second I hung up the phone, I started to feel a whole lot better.

3

UNFIT SOLDIER

S OMETIMES IT'S the unwritten rules that are the most important. But they are often the hardest to figure out and the hardest to follow. That's the way it is with the soldier's code. It says you're supposed to have your fellow soldier's back at all times. It may not be written on a plaque or in a training book, but it's in a soldier's DNA. In the army, there's nothing worse than being called a rat. A rat is the kind of guy who you can't trust and who's always reporting you up the chain of command for some stupid thing or another. Rats are vermin. They carry disease. In the army, rats don't last long. Real soldiers exterminate them.

I quit my job at the auto plant on September 15, 1997, and headed for Petawawa to report for active duty as a soldier with the first battalion of the Royal Canadian Regiment (1 RCR).

One of the first men I met there was the regimental sergeant major. I sat across from him in his office as he went through my file, figuring out where I'd fit.

"You're going into Charles Company," I was told. I didn't realize it at the time, but Charles Company was training to deploy to Bosnia, where Canada had active peacekeeping troops.

I was issued my Royal Canadian Regimental cap badge for my beret and a bag of gear. Then I was sent to another building, where I asked a clerk to watch my stuff for a few minutes while I registered.

"Sure," he said.

Ten minutes later, I returned to the clerk's desk, but he wasn't there. Neither was my gear. Panic set in, but before I could act on it the sergeant strolled in.

"Looking for something?" he asked.

"Yeah, I left my kit here with the clerk. Now it's gone."

"One man, one kit," he said. "It's your kit and your responsibility to look after it, not the desk clerk's."

The sergeant left the room and returned with my gear a moment later. "Next time, don't leave your stuff lying around."

I realized then that some guys like to mess with the new soldiers on the base, especially newbies from the reserves.

The next day was a complete whirlwind. I met lots of new people in the unit. I can't say they were the friendliest bunch of soldiers I've ever come across, but there was a reason for that. Unbeknownst to me, for this peacekeeping mission, the military command had dictated that the unit accept 20 percent reservists, despite having plenty of soldiers who could deploy. This meant that some of their own guys weren't going to Bosnia, and they were pretty pissed about it. This was also politics of regular versus reserve army, and I was sort of caught in the middle. I used to be in the militia, but now I was reg force RCR. From the perspective of troops in my new unit, I was a part-time soldier trying to muscle into their territory when they would have preferred that my spot be given to one of their own. And to top it off I hadn't even gone through the right of passage to be a "Royal" by going to RCR Battle School at CFB Meaford. They called guys like me cartoons—because to them we weren't real. RCR guys used to say to militia guys, "Your hobby is my career," which pretty much sums up their attitude. Of course, I wanted my hobby to *become* my career, but that wasn't so easy. One of the first things my new section commander said to me was something like "So, what good are you?" This strange dynamic didn't make for a smooth start. He was much shorter than me, and of course had a moustache. And I would learn that he wasn't much liked by most troops junior to him because he allegedly had a temper and a self-serving attitude.

When physical training began at 7 a.m., I showed up wearing shorts and a T-shirt.

My new sergeant looked me up and down. "Where the fuck is your RCR T-shirt? You better have a fucking RCR T-shirt tomorrow!"

Apparently, every RCR unit had its own kit shop, where guys could buy everything from RCR pens to RCR hats to . . . RCR T-shirts. I was supposed to have been issued a free RCR T-shirt when I arrived, but I definitely was not issued one.

Once the public blasting was over, the platoon went on a big run, about fifty guys on a 6.5 kilometre trek on a dirt road. Halfway through, we stopped at an exercise station with chin-up bars.

"Get up on those bars and give twenty chin-ups, troops. Now!"

As soon as we were finished that, the next order was shouted. "Did I tell you start running? I don't think so. Down in the dirt, soldiers. Fifty push-ups. Go!" And on it went. So much for a leisurely jog.

By the end of it, I was so physically drained that I was choking back vomit. I rushed behind a car in the parking lot so no one would see me puke. As I doubled over, I thought to myself, "I'm twenty years old and I chose this. What the hell am I doing?" This was a far cry from my cushy job on the assembly line. A couple of guys spotted me, and they pointed and laughed. "Ha-ha, check out the new guy!" As I spilled my guts all over the pavement, I knew I was in tough.

•

I may not have been the best runner in the group, but I knew one thing: I was a good shot. I was excited to show off my stuff on the range. There was just one problem: I hadn't fired a rifle in about a year and a half.

The platoon headed out to the range. We had our rifles ready and we were given our ammo.

"With a five-round magazine, load. Ready!"

We cocked our rifles, putting bullets in the chambers, and put the safeties on.

"Targets to your front. On your time, go on!"

A few minutes later, after we'd finished firing our five rounds, the range safety NCO called, "Cease fire! For inspection! Clear weapons!"

The soldiers around me began taking out their magazines, pulling the bolts all the way back to lock them in place. But I couldn't remember those steps because it had been so long.

A corporal approached me. "Hey man, are you going to let me inspect your weapon so we can move on to the next relay?"

"Yeah," I said. "I'm just trying to remember exactly what to do here. It's been a while."

"Wait a minute, didn't you do your weapons handling test the other day?" The corporal was referring to a review that soldiers did, to refresh them on all the steps involved in shooting.

"No. I just got here yesterday."

"Oh, okay," he said. "I'm just going to take that," he said, grabbing my weapon. Then he called out, "Hey Sergeant, this guy didn't do his training."

My section commander, excited to have a new reason to yell at me, said, "Who didn't do the training? Who doesn't know how to use a rifle?"

"Mitic," the corporal replied.

"Mitic? I should have known." He turned to me. "Why the fuck didn't you do this training?"

The whole line of soldiers was staring at me now. Wasn't it his responsibility to tell me what training I had to do and when I should do it?

"I wasn't here when the others trained," I said. "And no one said I had to do anything."

"Okay, let's go," he said, and escorted me off the range. He called another corporal over, who set me up for the handling tests and delivered a few more choice words about what he thought of me.

Once my sergeant left the scene, the corporal said, "Sorry that happened to you, but you gotta know this shit, and if you don't . . . well, you saw what's going to happen. So let's just get through this and then you can get back there and shoot with the rest of the guys."

He quickly put me through my paces, and now that I had a chance to actually focus, all my training came back to me. I remembered how to operate the weapon—magazine unseated, double feed to the chamber, empty magazine. After a bit more practice, the corporal said, "Not bad, Mitic. You can get back out there and zero your rifle."

So I went back to the line and joined the other men. I still knew how to shoot. I was hitting the target consistently, but that didn't seem to matter.

"Back at it, are you?" some guy quipped.

Another one said, "Hey, new guy. Aren't you the one who didn't know how to unload his weapon?"

That's pretty much all it took. From that moment on, I was labelled as the guy who "didn't know how to unload his weapon." It took a while to shake that off.

•

A couple of weeks later, we had to do the Battle Fitness Test (BFT), which included a 13 kilometre march carrying all our gear. I got ready alongside everyone else, making sure I was properly packed and that all my equipment was clean and functional. It was time for inspection.

"Mitic!" my sergeant yelled. "What the fuck's going on with your bootlaces? You trying to be an individual?"

I looked down. I didn't see what the problem was. That's when I learned that while my boots were laced, they weren't laced right for RCR. I was taught "the Royal lace," and to this day, I lace all my boots and shoes like a good Royal.

That march was two and a half hours long and was gruelling because I was so out of shape. Even with my boots laced properly, I ended up getting all sorts of blisters. My feet had gone soft working the assembly line, and wool socks in army boots can be tough on the skin. I pulled my groin during the march, and I strained both my hamstrings, too. Put all that together and let's just say that I was a bit of a mess when I finished the test. That evening, I was in so much pain that I went to the base medical clinic to get attention for my blisters and strains. The nurse and the doctor seemed surprised to see me.

"What are you doing here?" they asked.

I explained to them that I'd suffered some minor injuries during the Battle Fitness Test and could barely walk. They asked for my name and unit, which I supplied. Then they fixed up my feet, piercing the blisters to remove the fluid, disinfecting them and issuing me some Tylenol.

At morning parade the next day, our section 2IC came up to our section.

"Hey Mitic, how are your feet feeling this morning?"

"A lot better, Master Corporal. I went to the base hospital last night and they fixed me up."

"And who gave you permission to do that?"

"Nobody. What do you mean by permission?"

"Mitic, this is the army. You need permission for everything," he said. "You realize this is going to be a problem."

"Well, I do now."

I had a hunch he was going to tell my sergeant, the same one who had been my biggest fan since my very first day in the unit. Sure enough, after the morning parade—and in front of everyone—my sergeant ripped into me.

"You don't just go to the fucking doctor by yourself around here! You got that, soldier? *We* decide when you've got a real medical problem!"

I was fuming on the inside, and all I wanted to do was defend myself or at least lash out against the stupidity of it all, but I kept my mouth shut. As the weeks went on, I was getting more and more eager to head back home to Brampton on the weekends to relax and unwind a bit. Of course, no one told me I needed a leave pass for that—yet another thing we didn't have in the reserves—but lucky for me, this was one of the only things my sergeant didn't find out about.

What he did know was that after our training, our company was slated to head to Bosnia. Because I was a direct entry, my contract stated that if I was found lacking, I could be sent back to battle school to redo infantry basic training instead of going overseas on a mission. It was up to my sergeant and the other higher ranks to decide. I most definitely didn't want to be sent back to training. It would mean a sixteen-week course where I would be treated like a fresh recruit yet again—not a soldier with experience. Going to Meaford to do basic could be interpreted only in one way: as a punishment.

The sergeant called me over one day. "You're going to the rear party, to Alpha Company. And then you're going to Meaford."

"What?" I said. "Why?"

"Because that's the decision that's been made."

I was totally bitter about this. Charles was the company slated for Bosnia, and I was no longer a part of it. I trained with Alpha for another month and a half after that, but I was treated like a misfit. I got known as "the guy who got kicked out of Charles."

I was at the range one day helping to set up targets for the guys who were going to Bosnia. I went to my platoon warrant and said, "Why is this happening? I want to redress."

"You're not going to redress anything," he said. "You're going to suck this up and redo the training."

There was nothing I could do to change that decision: I had been deemed an unfit soldier. I was being sent to Meaford. So I went.

Being at Meaford was an exercise in torment. I was pissed off and my attitude didn't help matters. Order was everything there. Our boots were to be on one shelf, and one shelf only. Our toothbrushes and combs could not be beside our boots, so they had to be placed on another shelf. And not just any way, either. They had to be placed at a certain angle. I had to learn all of this from scratch and in a hurry, because it wasn't the same as I'd learned in the militia. Once I had everything in order, I shut my locker and prepared for lights-out.

The next morning, we were woken up at about five for a bed inspection. Sergeant Ironside did the inspection. I know it sounds like I'm making that name up, but I assure you it's real.

Sergeant Ironside, with the coolest army name ever, studied the name tag on my uniform. "Ah. You're Mitic. I've heard all about you. And now they've sent you to me. What *the fuck* should I do with you?"

I was about a foot taller than he was and couldn't help but look down at him. I said, "You can do whatever *the fuck* you want with me, Sergeant."

As soon as the words were out of my mouth, I regretted them. They surprised everyone in the place, but I swear they surprised me the most. The whole room got quieter.

The sergeant took a step back and looked up at me, one eyebrow raised as though this were very amusing. "Really. So it's going to be like that?"

That one sentence, one stupid sentence that came barrelling out of my big mouth, fucked me up for the rest of the course. Sergeant Ironside decided to make sure I regretted it from that day forward, and I don't blame him for it.

•

Training at Meaford included a basic infantry course that taught soldiers how to handle weapons, how to take cover and how to do things like dig a trench and live in it. It was brutal because it was wintertime in Meaford, which is out on Georgian Bay, on Lake Huron, but apart from that, the actual training was now child's play to me. I already had experience doing all of that stuff. Of course, that didn't stop me from getting in shit, no matter how well I was doing at the actual skills. I stepped in shit even when there wasn't any to step in. One time I was doing a fitness run and crossed the finish line with a smile on my face because I was surprised by how fast I'd completed the run. I got in crap for being too happy. Shit-eating grin took a new meaning at that point. I got accused of being a smug know-it-all. It seemed like a no-win situation.

At some point during our basic training, we headed down to London, Ontario, for something called citizenship training. The idea was to do research at the RCR museum, to soak in the history of the regiment and connect with real articles from the past. That's what we did during the day. At night, we hit the town.

In all fairness, those nights were more than just an excuse for a good time; they were a great way to form bonds with the other recruits. One night, a bunch of us ended up at a strip club. I was having a great time, until one of the recruits I was getting to know turned to me and said, "This is boring. Let's get some blow."

Blow? I'd never done serious drugs in my life. "Why the fuck do you want to get coke?" I asked. "Let's just stay here and have some drinks."

"Come on, bro, it's awesome. You'll take it and feel like the coolest guy in the room."

A big part of me wanted nothing to do with it. But there was another part of me that thought back to the soldier's code. Weren't we always supposed to have our comrades' backs? Weren't we supposed to fight together and play together? And if this guy went out on his own and something went wrong, who would help him then?

I reluctantly followed my friend, probably not one of my better decisions. We ended up meeting someone who offered to take us to a place to get coke. I took one look at him and knew right away this was trouble.

"Look, we shouldn't be doing this," I told my friend. "Let's just back out now and go back to the club."

But this dude was hell-bent on getting his coke, so I went along with him for the ride to keep an eye on him and hopefully keep him out of trouble. We got into a cab and stopped somewhere to pick up two long-haired weirdos. As I looked out the window, I thought about what a stupid situation I'd got myself into. Just an hour earlier, I was at a bar, having a great time, and here I was now jammed up in a cab with total losers. We drove to some dive on the edge of town and hopped out. We went inside and I stood by the bar while my buddy went into a booth with these guys. A few minutes later, he came up to me and said, "I got the stuff. Let's roll."

"The sooner, the better," I said, downing the rest of my warm, flat rye and ginger.

We had barely stepped out of the place when we were tackled by a couple of big guys. It all happened so fast. Suddenly I was on the ground yelling, "I'm not going to fight! Just don't wreck my jacket!"

I was wearing a nice leather jacket, and for some reason, all I could think of in that moment was how I didn't want it ruined by rolling around on gravel and pavement. The next thing I knew, one of these guys was slapping handcuffs on me.

"Got any ID?" he asked as he pinned me to the ground.

"Sure," I said. "Front pocket." My buddy was receiving similar treatment from the other guy. When they scanned our ID, they said, "You two are in the fucking army? And you're buying crack?"

My brain was exploding. "Crack! What are you talking about?"

"Stay calm," my friend said, like he'd been in this situation a million times. Right. Calm. He'd just bought crack from a two-bit dealer on the edge of town and we'd just been caught by the cops! I wanted to strangle him, and I was so pissed off at myself. I felt like a fool.

They tossed us in cells at the London police headquarters and did a strip search. Later, they put me in front of an investigator.

"So our undercover officers said you had nothing to do with this buy. Did you know what your friend was doing?"

"Yeah, I knew what he was doing," I responded. "But I was just there to have his back in case something went wrong. I didn't even want to be there."

"That's the impression our guys got. They said you didn't say a word in the cab, didn't participate in the transaction. They said you're just dumb for being there. Dumb and lucky—we're not charging you with anything."

It was a relief to hear. "So I can just go now?"

"It's not quite that easy. We'll take you back to your unit."

"So, the chances of the army not finding out about this are basically zero, right?"

No answer. They drove me back to the barracks and the cops knocked on the door. One of the NCOs came out.

"Mitic, what are you doing here?"

A cop spoke before I could. "We arrested him and another of your guys for purchasing narcotics. We're letting Jody go because he didn't actually do anything, but we still have your other guy at the station. And we may charge him."

My superiors were angry and disappointed. My platoon commander said, "I get that you backed your friend up, Mitic. But I can't condone that when he was buying drugs. I don't know what to tell you."

Eventually, my friend was brought back as well, and the next day, all of us recruits were bused back to Meaford. But now my friend and I weren't allowed to wear civilian clothes or a uniform. Instead, we were given one-piece grey overalls, the kind mechanics wear. We got on the bus and were sent to the back. We were ordered not to talk to anyone, which didn't really matter because no one would have talked to us anyhow. I felt and looked like a loser.

Back at Meaford, we were marched into the barracks. We had to clear out all our gear from our rooms and we were moved to another building, to PAT platoon—Personnel Awaiting Training. Basically, when you're in PAT platoon, you're the "bitch of the base." If there's some GD—general duty—no one else wants to do, PAT is going to get stuck doing it.

A few days after arriving, I got called to meet with the platoon commander. He sat me down and levelled with me with his best guess of what was going to happen now. "Basically, what the army is trying to do is release you guys as fast and easily as possible. Let's face it, if it was pot, maybe this wouldn't be such a big deal. But this was crack. And a lot of it!"

"So what does that mean?" I asked.

"Just have to wait and see."

But days went by and I just waited and waited and waited. There were no answers. It seemed nobody knew what to do about this case.

One day I was told I could stay in the Forces, and the next I would hear I was on my way out.

I was in the mess hall eating lunch one day when I overheard the base adjutant officer explaining the situation to some visiting officers. "Did you hear about the soldiers busted for drugs? And not just any drugs—crack!" I cringed just hearing him describe it. "Now we're trying to sort out the paperwork to get those two guys out of the army as fast as possible."

I couldn't believe what I was hearing. Usually there was a process for this kind of thing—you get charged, you have a court case, then your fate with the army is decided. But this guy was suggesting I might be facing dishonourable discharge without any process at all.

The base commander called me to his office shortly after that. "Mitic," he said, "when a fellow member displays misconduct or does something illegal, your duty is to report it." He told me I'd violated section 129 of the National Defence Act, engaging in conduct unbecoming to a soldier.

"But sir," I said, "I just wanted to protect him from himself. That's the only reason I was at that bar with him. We all talk about how we're supposed to stand up for each other and not rat each other out. I was trying to do the right thing. The soldier's code. I was trying not to be a rat."

"That's pathetic," the base commander said. "You're a disgrace to the uniform and to my regiment. If it were up to me, I'd kick you out of the army right now. But it's not up to me. You're Petawawa's problem, so I'm going to let Petawawa deal with you. Now get the fuck out of my office and off my base!"

When I left the base commander's office, my car was already packed. All my gear was inside it and a recruit from PAT platoon handed me my keys while avoiding eye contact. I'd been ordered to show up at Petawawa as soon as possible, but it was a Friday, so I headed to my dad's for a weekend visit instead. Fuck it. I was already in shit, so what did a few more days matter to anyone?

"What are you doing here, my son?" Dad asked when I arrived.

"Oh, I had the weekend off," I lied, "so I thought I'd come by for a visit." I was so ashamed I couldn't bring myself to tell him the truth.

On Monday morning, I showed up at the base in Petawawa, not knowing exactly how to proceed. I went up to the duty sergeant in the reception of our battalion building. "Hey, I'm Private Mitic. I'm back from Meaford," I said.

He looked me up and down. "Oh yeah. Hey, Fuckie! They're expecting you."

He took me upstairs to meet with the drill sergeant major—the DSM—who laid into me about what a good-for-nothing piece of crap I was, just in case I was confused about this point. I was assigned a new barracks room and put on the DSM's staff. Hardly any of the guys from the battalion would talk to me. I'd show up for morning parade, and afterwards I'd wait in the hall outside the DSM's office for whatever general duty—read "shit job"—would be given me. For the next nine months—probably the worst of my entire life, even to this day—I worked at shit jobs for the DSM and awaited my fate, which seemed to change every day. My case went to a senior committee of the regiment for review, and in the meantime, I heard varying reports on what would happen. It was like Meaford again. One day I'd hear all was forgiven and things were going to be fine. The next I'd hear that the Armed Forces wanted to cancel my contract.

One of the few guys who took the time to talk to me properly was the regimental sergeant major, who everyone called Uncle Billy. He was this little wiry dude who carried around a tomahawk whenever he was in the field training. Uncle Billy had seen and done it all. He was everything a regimental sergeant major is supposed to be—tough, smart, experienced, feared, and respected by all: a soldier's soldier. I loved him even though he scared the shit out of me every time he walked by. It didn't matter that he was half my size. Uncle Billy's office wasn't far from where I was posted, and he passed me every day in the hallway.

"Mitic," he'd say, looking straight into my soul.

I'd spring to attention, hope he was in a good mood and bark, "Sir!" Chief warrant officers like Uncle Billy, even though they are NCOs, have earned the right to be called "sir."

This went on day after day, and after a while we got into more conversation. One day, he said, "Mitic, how are you doing, soldier? How is everything going?"

Wait, I thought. Did he just call me "soldier"? "Sir! Good, sir," I said. "I've got no problems at all." I was bullshitting and he knew it, but I wasn't about to complain to a guy like Uncle Billy.

"Any news yet from the brass?" he asked, even though he probably knew more than I did.

"Not yet, sir," I said. Then one day, nine months after that night in London, a report came in from a senior committee of the regiment saying that the London police had not charged me with anything and that, as a result, the Canadian Armed Forces felt that there was no need to proceed with further action against me. I was allowed to stay in the army.

But at this point, I was so disillusioned by everything that had happened, I decided I didn't want to stay anymore. I let that be known. The colonel I spoke to said, "Fine. You want out, then we'll prepare your release. It'll take a few weeks to come through, and then you're done."

That was fine by me. I continued to report to the DSM while I waited to get my walking papers and be released from the army forever.

One day, as I was waiting in the hallway, Uncle Billy came by.

"Come on over here," he said, leading me to a wooden bench, where we both took a seat. "I heard you want out."

"Yes sir," I said.

"But you've been exonerated of any wrongdoing. Are you sure that's the path you want to take?"

"Absolutely, sir," I said. "My dad has some big plans for me to do some business with him, and I might go back to my old factory job. Or maybe I'll go back to school. There are all sorts of things I can do," I said, though I felt completely full of it.

"It would be a real shame if you did that. Mitic, I've been watching you here. You're a good soldier. You've got what it takes. You've been a man about everything that happened. You show up here every day. You never denied anything." He paused. "I have a feeling this has been the worst time in your life."

"It has, sir," I said. I wasn't about to deny that.

"I really think you should reconsider your decision. This is a chance to try again."

Shortly after that conversation, a message came from the same senior committee that had reviewed my file previously. They stated quite frankly: "When we said Private Mitic was exonerated, we never said he could be released from his three-year contract. He will carry out his three-year commitment to the regiment." Whether I wanted to or not, I was going back to Meaford.

Uncle Billy's words came back to me in that moment. Here it was, my chance to try again. For a week, I debated with myself. I had two choices. I could be pissed off forever and feel hard done by, or I could go back to Meaford with a new attitude and make the best of it. I could keep my head high, get off the bus with the shiniest boots, the best-pressed uniform, the best-laid-out kit and the best attitude and be in the best shape of anybody there.

I took hold of my second chance. That's what I did. And I returned to Meaford to finish my training.

The second I arrived, I ran into Sergeant, now Warrant, Ironside. "So, Mitic. You're back—again."

I stood ramrod straight in front of him. "Yes, Warrant. No more bullshit, Warrant. No more fucking around."

"The colonel's not very happy to see you back on this base," Warrant Ironside said.

"I can understand that, Warrant. But I'm here to do my time and to learn what I need to. Then I want to earn my place in the regiment."

"Well, you've got a hell of a job ahead of you," he said. I wasn't sure, but I thought I detected a slight softening in the steely set of the sergeant's chin.

For the next three months, I was a model citizen and a perfect soldier. When the training ended, I graduated as a top candidate, and I was the top marksman as well. For the top shot, I got a little trophy with my name on it. To this day, this remains one of my proudest accomplishments.

At the graduation parade, the base commander who had previously told me I was a disgrace to the army came up to me and shook my hand. "Keep it up, Mitic. We need more Royals like you. You're going to be good for the regiment." Big smile, firm handshake.

So what did all this mean? What did it amount to? I would now have a chance to show off my stuff in Kosovo. I was sent on my first overseas deployment.

4

NOT FIT TO SHOOT A DOG

I HAVE A distinct memory of my dad crying in the parking lot of a Jack Astor's restaurant in Brampton about a week before Christmas in 1999.

I was headed for my first overseas deployment—a six-month assignment for peacekeeping in Kosovo. Canadian peacekeepers formed part of the NATO-led Kosovo Force—KFOR—and had deployed on June 12 that year, two days after the adoption of a UN Security Council resolution. At the time, Kosovo was facing a dire humanitarian crisis, with military forces from the Federal Republic of Yugoslavia and the Kosovo Liberation Army in daily conflict. Serb forces were engaged in a mission of ethnic cleansing against Kosovar Albanians. By this point, the death toll was rising rapidly, and an estimated one million people had fled Kosovo as refugees.

My dad watched the news; he knew what was going on there. And on that day, my dad took me and one of my friends to Jack Astor's for a farewell meal. He was quieter than usual all through the meal. He was pushing his food around on his plate. When we were in the parking lot afterwards, I gave him a big hug, and his emotions got the better of him.

"Look, I'm only gone for six months, Dad," I said, trying to reassure him. "Think of it as six haircuts. Or six credit card payments. That's not really a long time."

He tried to smile through his tears, and I'll never forget the look in his eyes as he tried to say goodbye and keep his fears to himself. At that moment, the saying "You might volunteer to be in the army, but your family is drafted" became real to me.

But as for the military aspect of heading overseas, I felt ready. I was prepared for this mission and I had thoroughly enjoyed the training exercises leading up to our deployment. It was totally different to train for a mission than to just train for the sake of training. There were pairs fire-and-movement drills, live grenade-tossing practices and elaborate live-fire combined arms training exercises. My job in this section was a C9 machine gunner.

We started with single-person drills, then moved on to pairs, then to section, then to platoon, until by the end of training, we practised as an entire battle group of hundreds of soldiers and tanks and artillery, all moving together to attack the enemy with live ammunition. It was incredible stuff. The final exercise was meant to simulate an attack on a Russian/Warsaw Pact defensive position, and we were to work together to approach and overwhelm the trenches up ahead. Each tank was supported by a platoon of infantry in four armoured vehicles. When you're dismounting and running next to a tank, you have to stay behind the second road wheel of the tank. You can't go too far forward, because when the tank fires the main gun, the concussion could knock you out or kill you. I was pumped!

So the tanks moved forward, firing at the targets with their main cannons and coaxial machine guns. Then the infantry fighting vehicles pulled up on an angle, forming a wall of armour. All of us infantry guys jumped out the back of the vehicles and fanned out behind our platoon's tank, using our vehicles as cover until we were in position. Meanwhile, the section commander grabbed a handset phone at the back of the tank. This phone was on a fifty-foot cord and allowed communication with the tank commander so the speed of attack could be coordinated.

As we moved in, the tank fired its main gun, which exploded loudly each time. A dismounted anti-tank team with a Carl Gustav anti-tank rifle was on the far right flank and was sending in anti-tank missiles. It was awesome. Everything was blowing up around me and I couldn't believe it was actually happening. After a while moving forward, we made it to the Russian defensive line, home of the imitation enemy. Russian trenches are dug in zigzags. Now we had to overtake the trench.

I was using a C7 for that drill, not a C9, and I'm better with a C7. Like all the infantry, I had live grenades and was covered in ammo. The first guy forward had to run up to one of the zigzag trench corners. He crawled to the edge of the trench, threw in a hand grenade and yelled, "Grenade!" The grenade exploded, then his partner jumped forward and sprayed bullets into the trench. Then the first guy jumped into the trench to cover that corner.

Now it was time to secure the next part of the trench. It was my partner, Barry, and me. We approached the next corner and Barry tossed in a grenade. As soon as it exploded, I jumped around the corner, spewing a full thirty-round magazine of ammo. During all this exercise, range safety guys, also known as umpires, were coming up to us to say, "You're out. Dead. You've been hit," or, "You're a casualty. Get down on the ground." Barry got taken out by an umpire at this point, but I was still alive, so I ran up around the next corner and reloaded.

Another one of the guys came running up behind me and jammed the cold metal barrel of his rifle right into my back. In my head I was thinking, "That's live ammo. I could die right here and now. By friendly fire." This soldier was so in his zone he didn't even notice where his rifle was pointing. I knew if I turned quickly and startled him or if he flinched when the grenade went off, he might shoot, so I just kept doing what I was supposed to do. I pulled the pin from my grenade and threw it around the next corner. Fortunately, the guy didn't shoot me when the grenade blast washed over us and I didn't accidently die. We continued on down the trench until the entire stretch of it was overtaken and we poured out the far end, knowing it was clear of the enemy. Everything had gone as planned, and the exercise—the most incredible one I'd experienced so far—was a success. At the end, we were high-fiving, totally stoked by everything we'd just done.

That's one example of the very cool things we got to do in training. And at the end of it, we were in the drill hall when the commanding officer told us the news. "Soldiers, you are ready to be deployed to Kosovo. We will be the second rotation, relieving the first group deployed earlier this year."

I recall the feeling of excitement that swept through my body. This was the reason I had signed up to be a soldier—to serve on missions. Suddenly all the exercises I'd just completed took on a different meaning. This wasn't fun and games anymore. I said to myself, "This is the real thing. I know what I'm doing." In my mind's eye, I saw myself take a grenade in my hand, felt the weight of it in my palm. I loved the feeling of holding a grenade, of raising my arm, aiming and throwing it around a corner. I loved jumping to one side, grabbing my rifle and shooting the enemy. Yes. I could do this. I'd done it over and over in training. I was ready.

I had finally put my previous trouble with the army behind me, and just a few weeks shy of my twenty-third birthday, I'd be on assignment in a foreign land—a peacekeeper.

But "peacekeeping" was a term that struck a lot of us soldiers as inaccurate, especially in this conflict. That word was true on some levels, because it defined a United Nations approach. But with NATO, our role wasn't so much the "keeping" as it was the "making"—we were more like "peace-makers" or "peace-enforcers," as we called ourselves. There's a lot of talk about why Canadian soldiers have such a good reputation for keeping the peace on the global stage. Basically, what makes Canadian soldiers different is that we stand our ground. When warring factions want us to move and are attacking us and actively campaigning to push us aside, we stay put and even shoot back, as our forces did in Croatia in the fall of 1993 in the Medak Pocket. The Croatian forces were trying to attack a village. Canadian and French troops defended the village, when usually UN peacekeepers would have gotten out of the way. *That's* "peace-enforcing," Canadian style.

Even though I was excited about the mission, I did have some misgivings. During the final stages of training, I started having trouble with my C9 machine gun. This is a belt-fed machine gun that can fire between eight hundred and twelve hundred rounds per minute, but mine was jamming every ten rounds. I'd get a few rounds out, and then it would jam. I'd have to clear the jam and reload before I could shoot.

I went to my master corporal. "My weapon isn't working," I said. "I think we need to send it to the weapons techs."

"Let's have a look," he said. He inspected the weapon. He couldn't find any obvious problem. We filled out the necessary work order and sent the gun off for fixing. When I retrieved it a few days later, there was a tag on it that read, "Not serviced due to uncleanliness." Apparently, the weapons tech didn't want to get his hands dirty. This is kind of like taking your car to the mechanic, only to have him say, "I'm sorry, but there's too much grease under your hood for me to fix your ignition. There's nothing I can do for you."

I took the gun and the note to the master corporal. "Check this out," I said.

He read the tag, then shrugged. "Don't worry about it," he said. "You're probably not going to be using that weapon in combat anyway."

That told me a lot. It meant this overseas mission would probably not involve a lot of action, which, I'll admit, was a bit of a disappointment. It's what I was best at. It's what I was really craving.

Because this was my first assignment, I was naive when it came to procedures. I was told to report to the Departure Assistance Group, or DAG, a team that makes sure you're ready to be deployed. I was asked a whole lot of questions. Some questions made sense: "Are your immunizations up to date?"

"Yes. All up to date."

Some were kind of ridiculous: "Do you have all your combat gear?"

"Well, yes, I do. Might come in handy."

And some brought the hard reality into focus: "Do you have a will?"

DAG also assesses a soldier's mental and physical fitness. It's the same principle as a traffic light: green for "good to go," yellow for "maybe, but we have some issues to resolve first," and red for "hell no—this guy's screwed." Red could mean a lot of things, like you weren't mentally well or you had a medical or family issue that made you unfit to be deployed.

Once I got the green light for departure, I was given a list of instructions, which included bringing six months' worth of personal supplies for the mission. Sometimes, DAG sounded a bit like your mom, and so it was when they told us, "Don't forget to bring extra soap and shampoo." A bunch of us who had never been overseas before stocked up like there was no tomorrow. I bought two massive bottles of shampoo, which in hindsight makes no sense given that

I only had a buzz cut's worth of hair on my head. On future assignments, I learned how to better manage my supplies.

We were issued two plastic barrack boxes each, which were about one foot deep and two feet wide. DAG told us what we could and could not bring. They even had traffic techs whose sole job was to scrutinize our boxes and make sure we'd packed properly. Once everything was checked, our bags were collected and shipped off before we were.

On December 20, 1999, we bused down to Trenton and flew out on an aircraft with a contracted airline. The plane felt like it was held together by duct tape and bubble gum. After a long and shaky flight to Ireland, we got on another flight to Greece. From there, we had a seven-hour bus ride to a village just outside Priština, the capital city of Kosovo.

Our dirt camp was next to an abandoned police station that allowed us to control the southern access roads to the international airport. There was a mess hall, three barracks and a shower tent. The shower worked only some of the time and the hot water was inconsistent at best. In the middle of our site was an old in-ground swimming pool that was no longer in use. Being Canadians, we quickly transformed that into a ball hockey rink so we could enjoy a little taste of home.

Our platoon commander was Eleanor Taylor, who would later become the only woman to lead a NATO combat unit in Afghanistan. She was a great soldier, one of the better officers with whom I've ever worked. She was also cute, but nobody messed with Taylor because she was as tough as fucking nails.

After a few days in camp, a routine set in for us. We were all looking forward to patrolling and engagement on the ground. I wanted to put my soldier skills to use, but it didn't exactly work out that way. Instead, we would patrol during the day for eight to ten hours. Then we'd hang out at night. Over and over again, day in, day out. Patrol. Hang out. Patrol. Hang out. Rinse and repeat.

After a few weeks of his, I was nearly banging my head against the wall. I was so bored, and so were the rest of the guys. Was this what being in the army was like? A whole bunch of waiting around, doing what any shopping mall security guard could do? We weren't putting our training into practice at all. It was all just walk, patrol, walk, patrol. There weren't even any real threats nearby to guard against.

I remember thinking to myself, "If this is what army life is like on overseas deployment, I'm going back home after this and applying to become a police officer." On our off time, we weren't even doing group PT to keep us physically sharp, which surprised me because I didn't think we were in great shape, and we were growing softer by the day. Some of us decided to take matters into our own hands.

We approached one of our commanders. "Sir, we're losing it here. Look at us. We're turning into couch potatoes. We've got to do something."

The response: our commander secured a bunch of bikes for us to ride around on. That's right, bicycles. We were military men and women serving on patrol, and we had fun riding our bikes around pretending we were tourists.

The days were getting colder as we approached the end of the year. Usually in Kosovo, the winters are fairly mild. You could get away with a leather jacket on top of a sweater. But, of course, since Canadians were around, that winter happened to be one of the coldest on record, with routine lows of minus 20 or 30. One night, the temperature actually bottomed out close to minus 60. "You guys are Canadian. You must be used to this," the Americans and British quipped, but we were freezing our asses off.

Being extremely cold and extremely bored, we were put on patrol on New Year's Eve of 1999. This was the year of Y2K, before any of us knew that the whole thing was a hoax. We were told to prepare for widespread chaos, looting and insurgency in the streets. Finally! This was our first real assignment, potentially our first opportunity to put our training skills to the real test. But when we got our marching orders for the night, we were in for a surprise.

"Okay," our major announced, "our objective for the night is to stop people from driving drunk."

"So . . . how exactly do we do that?" I asked.

"Well," the major responded, "you're to stop passing traffic and tell drivers not to drive drunk."

"Do we have the authority to detain them if they are drunk behind the wheel?" I asked.

"No."

Someone else asked, "Do we have Breathalyzer equipment to test drivers?"

"No."

"So we just have to ask them nicely not to drink and drive and send them on their way? Is that it?"

"Yes."

Great. So we were a glorified road check without any authority to act in the case of drunk driving. We headed out for this assignment feeling deflated, useless and unimpressed. Before I left, I was stopped by the company sergeant major.

"Mitic," he said.

"Yeah?"

"Ditch your name tag tonight."

"Okay. Why?"

"Because your last name is Serbian." This was an ongoing issue, because my dad is of Serbian descent. It was decided that for the tour, I'd use the name tag "Mitch," but I never did get that tag.

In order to avoid provoking an unwanted reaction, I headed out to patrol that night as an unknown soldier.

We trekked out to a crossroad south of the airport. There were no street lights, no stoplights, no sidewalks, nothing. Nothing at all for kilometres. We hunkered down and waited. It was mind-numbingly boring. We could see a car coming miles before it arrived. "Steady up, troops!" someone would say, dripping with sarcasm. "Here comes trouble."

Cars eventually pulled up, and most of the people we stopped spoke French. I spoke enough French to ask where they had learned it.

"Switzerland" was a common response. A whole bunch of educated foreigners were driving around on back roads, totally sober on New Year's Eve, probably as bored as we were.

"Don't drink and drive!" we'd say. And then they'd be on their way.

One time, we pulled over a car full of kids about my age. "Have you been drinking tonight?" I asked.

"Fuck yeah! It's the millennium! Woo-hoo!"

These kids were headed to a party, and I wished I was going with them. I was thinking about all my friends and family back home going to parties and having a great time. And here I was, stuck in the middle of nowhere on a freezing-cold night in Kosovo, serving as a roadside drunk-driving check.

We did see some gunfire that night, though—just not the kind we'd expected. At midnight, all the anti-aircraft guns in the area fired their tracers into the air. They let go some celebratory para-flares, too. We had orders to report all gunfire in the area, so the master corporal picked up the microphone. "There are shots being fired right now. Oh, wait . . . There's more. Oh, and now I can hear machine guns. And there's the flares. Oh, to hell with this." He hung up the phone.

The Y2K stuff never materialized and we never had to deal with any dangerous individuals during our all-important roadside drunk-driving check program. That New Year's Eve in Kosovo was one of the most action-devoid that I had on my deployment. And the New Year didn't get any better in terms of excitement. It was followed by a few more dreary weeks of boredom.

If there was a glimmer of drama and tension in Kosovo, it was only because of the Russians. What were the Russians doing in Kosovo? There was lots of speculation, but no one really knew. Just before NATO arrived on the scene, the Russians took over a section of the Priština Airport and stayed there. Part of our job was to keep an eye on them. One rumour said they had a secret hangar on the side of a hill inside the airport perimeter and during the night they would launch planes from there. The Russians had lent aircraft to the Serbs to fight their civil war and they were flying those planes back home before anybody took an inventory. Others went as far as to suggest they were shuttling nuclear or biological weapons in and out of the area.

We had checkpoints near the Russian base, so it was convenient for us to keep an eye on them. We like to think that we're tough as Canadians, but it turned out this Russian unit were Russian airborne who had come from fighting in Chechnya. These guys took things to a whole new level. They were hard-core soldiers. We would complain when our showers weren't giving us warm water. Then we'd look over to the Russian camp and see soldiers outside in minus 25 degrees washing themselves with snow, or out in T-shirts cutting firewood. These guys were sleeping in World War II–era tents, while we were sweating inside our heated barracks. And every morning, they'd be outside in the ball-freezing cold, running, doing chin-ups and bench-pressing big truck tires.

A lot of the Russian army was made up of mandatory conscripts. As a result, they would often go AWOL, spending some time at the local bars and whorehouses as a way to escape the rigours of army life.

One night, a couple of Russian guys got drunk and ended up in one of their armoured fighting vehicles. It had a machine-gun turret on the top. These clowns were doing doughnuts and pointing their machine gun all over the place, including in our direction. Our anti-tank teams surveyed the situation closely and were poised to strike if that gun was pointed at us one more time. To this day, I'm sure those drunken soldiers had no idea how close they came to being blown up by our anti-tank missiles and causing an international incident.

Over time, we started to get to know some of the Russians better, and we came to enjoy hanging out with their guards. As a young soldier, I was always interested in hearing front-line war tales from older soldiers. Some of these Russian troops had fought in Afghanistan and in Chechnya. They'd been in some major combats. We were fascinated.

One time a group of us told these Russian soldiers how we stopped a car at a checkpoint and encountered passengers who would not comply with our orders. The Russian we were talking to was a guy in his thirties, a colonel. "Why didn't you just beat them?" he asked.

There was a pause. We were all waiting for a smile to creep across his face, but he was dead serious.

"We're actually not allowed to do that," we said.

"Why not? Aren't you the authority around here?"

We tried to explain that being aggressive wasn't an approach that Canadian peacekeepers turned to so quickly. "Doing something like that is our *last* resort," I said.

He looked at us coldly. "That's our *first* resort. When we aren't respected, we don't take it."

That Russian colonel went on to tell us how he and his men had dealt with insurgents in Chechnya, kicking people with steel-toed boots or shooting down vehicles that didn't stop at their checkpoints.

When we were in Afghanistan a few years later, these stories would echo in my mind. But not then, not in Kosovo. Because nothing was happening there at all. I continued to feel totally let down by how little we were contributing, and I was disillusioned by my very first time on operation.

One of a soldier's favourite pastimes is swapping gear with other soldiers. We Canadians had just been issued brand-new Gore-Tex jackets and fleece to get us through the cold winter. Once the American, British and Norwegian troops saw our fleece sweaters, they wanted to know how they could get their hands on some.

One British soldier came up to me and said, "Want my Gore-Tex jacket in exchange for your Gerber multi-tool?" Every Canadian soldier had been issued a Gerber, which was a better version of a Swiss Army knife. It had pliers, scissors, wire cutters and all sorts of things that were helpful in dismantling mines and explosives.

Allegedly, I pulled out the tool and made the trade because his Gore-Tex had cool reflective stripes. Once that deal went down, it was no holds barred. We traded jackets, toques and basically anything that we'd brought. But all of this had to be done on the down low, because trading gear with other countries' service people was strictly prohibited.

At one point, I was pretty sure I was going to get busted and reprimanded for my trades, because my warrant officer took note of some of my new gear. But that's not how it turned out. He was happy to see a soldier with a personable quality and good communication skills. He quietly sent me back to the British camp with a bunch of things he wanted me to trade for him.

Later, at the American compound, I saw this cool pair of sunglasses and decided I had to have them. I traded them for a piece of my gear. I loved those glasses. I thought they made me look like Maverick in *Top Gun*. I was cutting-edge. But when I showed off my new shades to my buddies, they said, "That's not a good look for you."

"Really?" I said.

"Dude, you look lame."

I ended up chucking out that pair of sunglasses.

•

While the Kosovo posting lacked excitement, I did get my first opportunity to experience an army getaway weekend. The R&R breaks are exactly what they sound like, with the emphasis on rest and relaxation, though sometimes there's a lot more relaxation and not so much rest. They're usually short getaways, two or three nights, to a predetermined destination.

My first time on R&R, we were going to Sofia, Bulgaria, by bus. We would stay in two hotels, one designated for officers and senior NCOs (a quiet, buttoned-down residence), the other geared towards younger guys who wanted to let loose and party a little bit more. It's no surprise that I picked the second hotel on the list.

Two male officers and a female one were leading us through this briefing. Suddenly the female officer started to get uncomfortable and she let one of her male colleagues handle the critical instructions for us.

We were told a cautionary tale about a Canadian soldier who had visited this spot a couple of months earlier and ran into a situation. He met a girl at a bar and took her back to his hotel, only to have the mafia follow her home once she left. They took her money and beat her up. The girl had to pay the price, not the soldier. Message received.

As soon as we got the green light to hit the town, a few of the guys said, "Let's go to McDonald's!"

I was incredulous, but laughed. "Guys, we're on leave in an Eastern European country and all you can think of doing is eating McDonald's?" That's soldiers for you. Such simple creatures.

They took off without me, while my buddy Graham Blackwell and

I hit a more traditional restaurant. We ordered some food and had a great time. When the bill arrived, we were blown away to find that the entire meal cost about ten German marks, the equivalent of six Canadian dollars.

We left twenty marks each, giving a healthy tip to the waitress who had served us all night. As we got up to leave the restaurant, the waitress chased us down. She couldn't speak English very well, but it was clear that she was trying to give us change.

"No, no. That's for you," I said, putting the money back in her hand.

Tears started to stream down her face. We were both shocked, until we discovered customers rarely tip in Bulgaria, because money is so tight for everybody. Unbeknownst to us, we had given this waitress about two weeks' worth of wages.

From that point on, we rolled through Sofia like we were the stars in a Puff Daddy rap video. The booze was dirt cheap and the clubs were full of gorgeous women. We jumped into cabs during the day and toured around to get a feel for the city. At one point, our cabbie took us to a sketchy part of town with graffiti all over the walls—NATO GO HOME! We quickly got out of that area.

We were getting the VIP treatment all weekend because the mafia had put out the word that nobody had better mess with the Canadians. We looked so different from Bulgarian men that it seemed we turned a lot of heads. There were other differences as well. At a bar one night, a girl said to us, "You know what the biggest difference between you guys and Bulgarian guys is?"

"No idea," we said.

"It's not just your looks. It's that you actually treat us nicely."

My first R&R experience is one I'll never forget. And it certainly helped lift me out of the doldrums of Kosovo—at least for a while.

•

It seemed like forever before I finally discharged a weapon for the first time in Kosovo, but even that didn't quite live up to expectations. We were staying at our vehicle checkpoint overnight, and it was freezing cold in our tents. Nobody wanted to get out of their sleeping bags for any but the most dire reasons, and even running heaters all night, we were frozen.

The whole area had been deserted when the locals were forced to flee, and they had left their dogs behind. There were large packs of roaming dogs looking for food and establishing their territory. With a fragile peace being established, people were slowly moving back into the region and trying to establish a regular routine. They were going to work and were out in the streets, and kids were going to school. But the dogs were still totally wild. Sometimes they'd stalk children, and one of our jobs was to keep these packs away from little kids. One morning, a few other soldiers and I were chasing a pack of dogs away from some children and one of the dogs ran into traffic and got injured.

Now we had a new problem on our hands. This dog was already predatory, and now it was at risk of becoming more fierce because it was hurt. There was only one thing to do. We had to put the poor dog out of its misery.

I'm six foot four, right-handed and have perfect vision, so I figured my buddy Jeff's rifle would be about right since he's got the same build as me. But I accidentally grabbed the rifle of another soldier, a guy about a foot shorter than me, left-handed and who wore Coke-bottle glasses. I couldn't have picked a worse-matching rifle if I tried. Every firearm has different calibrations based on the shooter. If you grab a rifle off the rack because you don't have time to find your own, you better grab a gun belonging to someone roughly your size.

I went to an elevated position where I could see the dog limping through the acres of open field in front of me.

I turned to my master corporal. "Scott, I've got a clear shot. It's now or never."

"Okay, go ahead and do it," Scott told me. "But don't miss."

I'm not a hunter. My training has all been based on how and where to hit a human target. Still, I knew that when trying to shoot an animal, you aim for its vitals. I aimed for just under the shoulder so I could take out its heart or lungs with a single bullet and end things quickly. But because the rifle was not personalized for me, I ended up hitting the poor animal in the wrong spot. I was a good six to eight inches off the target, which was awful not only because the last thing I wanted was for this dog to suffer, but because I was always considered to be one of the best shots in the unit.

I needed to get another shot into the dog to put it out of its misery fast. I ran down to the bottom of the road, lay down and took one more shot. Mercifully, that one finished him off.

Scott came up to me a few weeks later. "You know they almost gave me a court martial and sent me packing back home?"

"What! What for?"

As it turns out, the chain of command was angry that he'd allowed a private to shoot a rifle. Apparently, the dog should have been shot with a pistol, and not by a lowly private but by a master corporal. I'd been trained extensively in shooting. I was one of the better shots. Yet when it came right down to it, I wasn't trusted to take down a dog.

That ended up being the most armed action I saw in Kosovo, the only time I discharged a weapon with the intent to kill. And even then, I was told I was out of line.

Dear Dad   Feb 22, 00

   I got back from Sophia Bulgaria a couple of days ago.
It was the best time of my life! 3 days was not long
enough. I want to go back and spend at least a couple of
weeks. The women are beutiful and plentiful. The really
dug Graham and I because we are both tall and have
bright coloured eyes. And because we are nice to them. Some
thing Bulgarian guys haven't figured out how to be yet. The
living is cheap. The posh steak houses are cheaper than the
McDonlds! The bars are open all night and there is no such
thing as last call. Basicly its awsome. It makes me even
more anxious to go tour Europe. That starts on April 9 to 27.
I'll be dropping in to Germany around the 20-21. Who should I see
first? I haven't a clue. By the time I'm back from leave
most guys will be home. I guess its safe to tell you that
the tour has been cut short. I'll more than likely be back
by early May now. No promises but right now thats what it is
If your going to the UK in June maybe I'll tag along if
I'm still on holidays. What you think?
   Things are pretty quite here right now. The problems that
you are probably seeing on T.V. are North East of us in the
French and Brit sector. We are (my platoon) on camp security
now. It not bad. A little boring but it can't all be gravy. Better
than VCP thats for damn sure!
   Are you getting my mail? I was hoping to get my Maxim mags from you.
Also are all my bills being paid OK? Those checks I wrote and such.
Hows Grandma? I called her a while ago and she seemed fine.
What about everyone else? I hope everything is cool there.
Say hi to Marion for me and Cory. I sent him a B-day present. Did
it arrive all right? If its not there yet don't tell him its coming okay?
Hey! You guys want to go camping for a weekend in Algonquin park
when I get back? I think it would be fun.
   Gotta go. Sorry I don't write more but I really am busy. I'll try
harder. Love your SON JODY P.S. Take Marty for a spin for me.

PART
2

The more thou sweateth in training, the less thou bleedeth in combat.

—Richard Marcinko, SEAL Team Six

5

FOR A BIT OF COLOURED RIBBON

NAPOLEON ONCE said, "A soldier will fight long and hard for a bit of coloured ribbon." That statement was true in the 1800s and it remains accurate to this day.

When I returned from Kosovo in 2000, I was disillusioned. The Kosovo experience was so dull and boring that it didn't exactly make me excited about a future in the military. Had I made a mistake in thinking life as a soldier would be thrilling? Had I been fighting for a bit of coloured ribbon that wasn't so interesting to me? And if it wasn't interesting to me, was I really meant to be a soldier? All these questions were floating around in my mind when I returned home.

September rolled around and so did the termination date of my contract with the army. My old commanding officer submitted his verdict via a written report. He said he felt it was best for the army to part ways with me and not renew my contract. The problem wasn't my service; it was my previous involvement in the drug incident. My old ghosts were haunting me yet again.

I can't say I didn't feel bitterness about this. I did. It didn't seem to matter that I had been a loyal soldier for the past couple of years and had handled myself with utmost professionalism during my tour of duty in Kosovo. What was holding me back was one stupid decision I'd made years earlier and had regretted ever since. It felt like no matter what I did or how I acted in the present, I'd always be eyed through the lens of one mistake I'd made years ago. I recalled a time in the field in Kosovo when I stumbled across a journal with some notes one of my superiors had written about each soldier in the platoon. Written below my name were three words: "Charged for drugs." In the Armed Forces game of broken telephone, I was erroneously reduced to a druggy. That sentence travelled with me all the way to Kosovo and all the way back.

I tried to rationalize with myself. It's not like I was getting a dishonourable discharge from the Canadian Armed Forces; it was just that they were not renewing my contract. Still, if the Armed Forces don't want to retain you as a soldier, it's not like you can walk away with your head held high. I vowed to myself I'd do everything I could to change that. If in the end it didn't work, fine. But I wanted to leave with my chin up, knowing I'd fought for myself, and if I could fight for myself, maybe that meant I was fit to fight for others, too.

Together with Lieutenant Eleanor Taylor, who'd been platoon commander in Kosovo, my platoon warrant, my company sergeant major and a number of others were willing to vouch for me, I started a process to have the drug reference erased from my file. I was interviewed by the regimental sergeant major, who was the head of the NCOs at the time, and made my case. I wouldn't call it begging (I prefer to call it "creative grovelling"), but whatever it was, I made every effort to let my superiors know that I wanted to stay in the Forces and earn my way up the ranks. In the end, they decided to purge the incident from my official record. They also gave me a new three-year contract. I now had as much of a chance as anyone else to move up the ranks. I could start pursuing the goal of becoming a sniper without having to clear any extra hurdles. That was my real dream, the role I'd wanted for as long as I could remember.

But wanting to be a sniper is one thing. That didn't mean that suddenly I *was* a sniper or that my days suffering drudgery and boredom were over. Shortly after signing my new contract, I was sent on a field training mission to Marine Corps Base Camp Lejeune, in North Carolina. My whole regiment was excited about this because we were the one regiment being sent to train against a U.S. Marine unit in a series of simulated battles and exercises. This was going to be a great experience. Finally, I would be getting the kind of real training I craved.

But not everything turned out the way we'd hoped. For starters, we got placed in condemned barracks infested with mice and rats. There were no sheets or covers on the beds, and the drainage was so slow that we were up to our knees in water every time we tried to shower. The toilets were side by side, without dividers, which took some getting used to. We made the best of it all and even turned it into a joke: "A unit that shits together sticks together." Our barracks didn't matter much to us anyways. What mattered was the training.

We were looking forward to the force-on-force battle exercises we'd been told about back home. We'd be using specialized laser equipment that re-created a true battlefield and even simulated casualties. As it turned out, we didn't get anywhere near that equipment. Instead, we did regular drills, except that each of our sections, comprising eight soldiers, was joined by a few Marines.

We were also excited about a promised visit to the USS *Intrepid*, a battleship used by Marines on their overseas missions. We'd have a chance to observe the Marines on a simulated drill out on the open seas. Once on board, we were assigned sleeping cabins that were the size of a phone booth—with two bunks in each. If you were sleeping on the top bunk and you got up too quickly, you'd smash your head against the ceiling.

As for observing drills, well, there wasn't much observing to be had. And when you're inside a big ship like that for a few days, you can't help but get cabin fever. There was nothing to do other than eat and sleep. The commanding officer for our Canadian battalion seemed to be as underwhelmed with our lack of activity as we were. He decided to address the issue with the head of the Marine unit. I'm not sure how that went, but what I do know is that we were kicked off the ship shortly after he'd lodged his complaint. So much for our simulated battle on the open seas.

We were sent back to our crappy old barracks at Camp Lejeune, where, during our final days, we finally took part in a worthwhile— if somewhat rushed—simulated naval assault on the North Carolina beach. Before we set out by ship, my sergeant quickly gave us orders.

"We're leaving in two minutes," he said. "The admiral won't take it kindly if our asses aren't on his boat on time. Got it?"

"Sergeant," I said. "Do I have time to use the facilities before we begin this mission?" It wasn't the most opportune question, but I really had to go.

The sergeant gave me a look that could only be interpreted as "Don't fuck with me, Mitic."

So no bathroom for me.

Off we went onto the boats, and once we landed on the beach, we were finally properly and fully engaged in a fantastic and useful simulated drill. We practised our fire and movement. All the while, the only thing I could think was, "Mitic, don't shit your pants." But it was damn near impossible. I've never wished for a diaper more in my life than I did then. And just when things were totally unbearable, I landed on a spiky plant as I dove to the ground and was forced to continue battle drills with a hand full of thorns and clenched butt cheeks.

Once we cleared the objective about twenty minutes later, I was beyond thankful when I heard the words "Re-org, re-org!" which meant we would regroup to assess supplies, casualties and missing soldiers. The platoon gathered in a circle, and I spotted my chance to sneak away while everyone else was busy redistributing ammo and supplies.

I ran to some nearby woods and dropped my pants. I could still hear the sounds of simulated gunfire in the distance, a sound that was far enough away not to be a threat and instead provided some lovely background accompaniment to my private moment. It was only once I was finished that I thanked my lucky stars I was carrying an American ration kit, because in the bottom of it was a tiny rectangular bundle of paper we called a toilet ticket. Once you unwrapped that minuscule packet, it magically transformed into enough toilet paper for at least one sitting.

I was a whole lot more relaxed as I sauntered back to the platoon. All the guys were laughing.

I gave a big thumbs-up and yelled, "Good to go!" as I took up my proper position in the re-org.

I thought I was going to North Carolina to learn tactics and strategy, to simulate intense battles and practise armed combat, but as it turned out, the most important lesson I learned was that I could hold my bodily functions for over two hours. And believe it or not, this, too, is an important skill when it comes to sniping.

6

THE PATROLLING SPIRIT

W HEN WE got back to Canada after that trip to North Carolina, I decided to try out for my battalion's Cambrian Patrol team. This team competes in an international competition, Exercise Cambrian Patrol, held in Wales each year. Various countries send their best military reconnaissance teams to the rugged Brecon Beacons mountain range, the training ground for the world-famous British Special Air Service, or SAS. Over the span of a couple of days, soldiers are faced with all sorts of obstacles and competitive challenges. There is a tremendous amount of pride in competing at this event, and the team that scores top points walks away with a gold medal. I was excited about tryouts, and I gave them my all. Despite that, I didn't make the final cut, probably because I wasn't quite ready. I didn't yet have the degree of training necessary to compete at that level. Still, I was happy that I took away some important lessons. I was exposed to some new training techniques and tactics, and the whole experience made me realize that I absolutely wanted to enter the world of reconnaissance (what we call recce) and snipers.

But to be a sniper, I first had to be recce-qualified. That fall, I went down to Brockville, Ontario, for a full drill where we simulated occupying the town. I was in platoon headquarters, because I had just been promoted to corporal and was given some extra responsibilities. I didn't realize it at the time, but my platoon warrant, who had been an elite sniper himself and had overseas experience, was assessing me to see if I would make a suitable candidate to be a sniper down the road.

One day, he said to me, "Do you want to go on your recce course?"

Of course I did, but there's sometimes weird politics in the army. If one unit knows a soldier wants to leave to join another unit, they can put up barriers to stop him.

I told him, "Yes. Absolutely, I want to go on that course. But not because I want to join the recce platoon. It's only because I want the training."

The following spring, I was dispatched to a recce course with about twenty other soldiers. It was a difficult course and definitely not for everyone. The most important thing we learned was "the patrolling spirit." Very few soldiers have it. The patrolling spirit is the willingness to do what it takes to get the job done, regardless of your personal comfort. This means you have to be willing to sit still under all conditions—while it's hot or cold, while mosquitoes are biting you, while you're in mud and you're hungry and tired. It means that if you have to carry extra batteries for the radio because you're going to be in position for three days, you make room by bringing only one meal a day. No matter how uncomfortable the conditions are, you get the job done. That's the patrolling spirit.

The recce course also included simulations where a team had to put IEDs—improvised explosive devices—at strategically important crossroads. It was our job to stake out a secret spot in which we could observe them doing this. The point wasn't to catch them in the act and then attack. It was to watch—carefully. Then we had to write a detailed report about what we had seen, reconstruct a map model and make a presentation on our findings. We were tested on reporting minute details with a high level of accuracy, which is of course a critical element of reconnaissance.

One soldier I knew went out on simulations with a Ziploc bag filled with yarn and tiny plastic army men.

"What on earth is all that for?" I asked him.

"For recall and information exchange," he told me. "You'll get it when I report."

Sure enough, after the simulated mission, he took out his yarn and toy soldiers and explained—in perfect detail—exactly what he'd seen, who did what and how. And everyone in that room understood him better because of his props.

For the duration of the recce course, we operated in smaller groups. I was with three other guys—Dave, Glen and Jay. Dave and Glen were big guys, physically fit and basically the stereotype of "the military man." Jay, however, was a tiny, skinny, pale wisp, with a laid-back attitude and the appearance of a pushover. At first glance, all I could think was, "What the hell is this guy doing in the army, never mind in a recce course?" But appearances can be deceiving, and deception is a key factor in the stealth that makes a recce guy blend in.

Jay was very well equipped to be a member of the recce team; he just didn't look that way. One time we were in an area with rolling hills. There were five or six metre drops throughout the terrain—we call it "micro terrain" because it won't show up on the map—and our mission was to reach a certain location by a certain time to set up an observation post. Of course, we had to deal with all sorts of obstacles that made that goal extremely challenging.

The four of us were in a hiding spot among the hills taking a break and it was Jay's turn to keep watch for the enemy. The "enemy" in this case was a fellow soldier named Eric who'd been picked to play the part of the bad guy. Eric loved nothing more than to catch his platoon mates, expose their locations and make them look like idiots in front of all of the instructors and trainees. It gave him immense pleasure to tie up his platoon members with a rope and gloat about how good his recce skills were.

Jay was on the lookout for Enemy Eric, while Dave, Glen and I were taking a breather. Jay was up on a rock, surveying the hills all around him. He reminded me of a meerkat, skinny and inoffensive, perched up there waiting and watching for god knows what. Suddenly his head cocked to one side and he said, "Shhh. Quiet."

We knew enough about Jay by this point to pay attention to him. "Dude, we don't hear anything."

"There's a vehicle coming. I can hear it," Jay said.

I looked at Dave. "You hear anything?"

"Nope."

"Glen?"

"Not a fucking thing."

"What the fuck are you talking about, Jay?" I called up. "We don't hear anything."

"That's because you guys are deaf," he called down.

Even though we didn't hear anything, we decided to heed Jay's warning. We got into secure hiding positions. Sure enough, about three minutes later, we started to hear the distinct sound of an Iltis jeep approaching. It was Eric, doing a sweep. There's no doubt he would have spotted us were it not for Jay's supersonic hearing. His ears were the most advanced alert tool ever created. Here was a guy who looked like a rodent and would be blown over in a breeze, but he was in actuality a very well-disguised offensive weapon. I gladly would have him by my side on any mission—that's how valuable his hearing was.

I learned a lot on that recce course, and like the lesson of Jay, many of the things I discovered were counterintuitive and challenged my assumptions about what it meant to be good at reconnaissance. At the end of the course, Sergeant Steve Good, a grizzled old soldier with a walrus moustache and a wad of tobacco permanently lodged in his mouth, called me over. He had a reputation for being as hard-core as a soldier can be.

"Hey Mitic," he bellowed in his deep tobacco voice, "what's this I hear about you wanting to be a sniper?"

"Who said that?" I asked.

"Doesn't matter," said the walrus moustache.

"Well, yeah, I do want to be a sniper."

"Why?" He spat a chunk of tobacco out to punctuate the question. "I hope it's not just for the cool T-shirt. We got a lot of guys who aren't serious, and if we're sending you to sniper school, we have to know it's for the right reasons."

"I don't care about the T-shirt," I said. "I just want to be a sniper."

"Okay, then. What are you waiting for, Mitic? Get the fuck out of here."

I've never been so happy to be told to fuck off. Clearly, the word was getting out about my goals, and the higher-ups were starting to see that maybe, just maybe, I had what it took to be successful.

Returning to Petawawa after completing the recce course was one of my proudest moments. We were picked up by helicopter, and just like in the movies, they let us hang over the edge and look down at the base from high in the air. The choppers landed right in the middle of the parade square at our unit. They were making a big spectacle for everyone to see. They were saying, "Look at what these soldiers accomplished. This is what happens when you put in some hard work and dedication."

Even though I was up high in the helicopter, I imagined myself down there on the ground as a young private, looking up, aspiring to be the soldier in the sky coming back to all the fanfare.

7

LESSONS FROM SNIPER SCHOOL

How to Be a Sniper

1. Be patient.
2. Be invisible.
3. Stealth is a more powerful weapon than your rifle.
4. Maintain your position, no matter what.
5. Remember everything.

I'D PASSED one major hurdle—I'd completed my recce course. But that didn't mean I had a free ride to sniper school. There were all sorts of barriers I still had to get around to be accepted into the course. I wooed and begged, coerced and schmoozed my immediate command to get them to recommend me as a candidate. Ultimately, what clinched it for me was that my platoon warrant officer, who'd been keeping an eye on me for a long time, gave me his thumbs-up for the tryout. There were twenty-five guys at the tryout, all of us vying for the coveted few spots on the sniper course. It was sink or swim. There was no instruction, no pointers—just go. The other thing that was different was that we were being evaluated based on individual achievement, so we weren't paired up or working in units the way we were used to. This time, it was just me, and me alone.

On the last day of tryouts, it was time to go shoot. The guys were all pretty cocky, and I was no different. I'd won top marksman when I finished battle school in 1998 and I always made marksman when I did my annual personal weapons test, or PWT. But at sniper tryouts, the instructors apparently weren't happy with our performance. We were getting on the truck to leave the range when we were told the bad news: "Nobody shot marksman today except for Kerr." Kerr had been on the rifle team for many years and had lots of experience. "But," the instructor continued, "we know you guys all shot marksman on your PWTs . . . so we'll pick the top ten scores and we'll let you know who's in."

At the end of that day, all twenty-five candidates were brought into the recce platoon area. The sergeant said, "I'm going to call out the names of ten people. Those ten people will be starting the sniper course next Monday morning. The others will not." He started reading out the names, and with every one that wasn't mine my stomach sank a little deeper. Finally, around name four or five, I heard what I wanted to hear: "Corporal Mitic." I was in.

•

I reported for the sniper course on Monday morning. This course was the first in a new type that had been totally overhauled by the Canadian Armed Forces. During the peacekeeping time of the early 1990s, the Canadian military concluded that its sniper program was in danger of being cancelled if it didn't evolve to meet the needs of the new millennium. The military also realized that sniper training should be a priority because, beyond shooting, snipers can also work in surveillance and in cover. A top-notch group of eight snipers can sometimes do the job of over a hundred or more soldiers, which is why the military came to see snipers as a "force multiplier."

Sniper training isn't only about target practice and shooting. We tend to think of snipers as primarily marksmen, but I think I could take almost anyone out to a shooting range and make them pretty accurate shots after a couple of days of training with the right equipment. A true sniper is someone who's willing to do pretty much anything to accomplish the mission. The sniper has a particular mindset, and shooting is actually one of the easier parts of the role—even at its most difficult (like when you're taking a shot at 2000 metres). I've seen men at the rifle range who are amazing marksmen but who would be terrible snipers because they don't have the patience. They lack the ability to deny their own needs and to put the mission first. A true sniper will make himself uncomfortable just to make the shot.

So what goes into "accomplishing the mission"? There's also range estimation (knowing how to make your shot, estimating the size of what you're looking at and calling in artillery), observation (looking for small details and remembering and reporting them accurately), camouflage and concealment (knowing how to hide and what to look for when searching for a hidden enemy) and small-team tactics (operating and moving in a two-person team). And, of course, shooting. But before a sniper shoots, he first has to understand his rifle. In the sniper course, when our instructor took out a C3 sniper rifle and showed it to us for the first time, we were practically drooling.

"This is a modified Mauser bolt-action," he said. "It was designed for the Canadian Olympic shooting team in 1977, but our military bought extra for our sniper units as well. This rifle has a synthetic stock. It has a ten-power Unertl scope, a bullet-drop compensator good to eight hundred metres. It has three minutes of adjustment left and right and up and down, in half-minute increments. It has a five-round box magazine."

I was listening to every word he said, but it meant absolutely nothing to me at the time. All I wanted, and all the rest of the guys wanted, was to pick up that rifle and shoot with it.

The master corporal continued: "This rifle I just showed you—it's mine." He pointed. "Yours are over there." I turned and saw a bunch of rifle cases all lined up. "Each of those cases has a name on it. Go get your rifles."

I jumped up and went to find the rifle case with my name on it. I brought it back to my spot.

Once we were all back, the instructor said, "Open up the cases." Inside was the rifle, the cleaning kit, the cleaning rod. We were told to put the rifle onto the bipod with the action back. Then the instructor showed us how to take it apart. "It's very important to keep your gun clean. But remember this. A perfectly clean rifle will not shoot the same way as a dirty one. Consistency is what matters. Every time you clean your gun, I want you to do it the same way. Never less, never more."

We learned how to fill out our dope book. I have no idea why it's called that, but the dope book is a shooter's data journal. It's filled with critical information about every shot a sniper makes. It's where we record conditions every time we pull the trigger, including the date, the weather, the circumstances, the lighting, the humidity and any other factor that might affect the rifle and how we used it. "Your rifle is *your* rifle. No one else can change a thing on it." With that, the master corporal pulled out screws and little screwdrivers and made us take off the scopes. "Those scopes were set for the last guys who used them. Now you're going to learn how to make a rifle yours and yours alone."

We continued to break the rifle into its component pieces.

"Now, put those rifles back together." We spent the next two or three hours putting the rifles back together. Once we were done with that, we were taken to the range, where we learned the elaborate process of zeroing a sniper rifle, which made it possible to aim at a target accurately. Once that was set, our rifles could fire five rounds into a one-inch target at 100 metres.

That was day one on the range. We learned so much in that one day that it was completely overwhelming, but also hugely exciting. As the course continued, we took those same skills and honed them, learning how to shoot when crawling through rain, in mud, in bright sun, while judging wind and light and working with a spotter who was your partner. With more and more practice, we developed instinct, a deep understanding of our rifles, how they worked, or didn't, and how we could use them to make the shot.

Later, we moved on to cam (camouflage) and concealment training. Our instructors took our group into the field. We were decked out in our ghillie suits—uniforms covered in camouflage netting and scrim. The ghillie suit is one of the things that makes a sniper a sniper. A good ghillie suit helps him blend into his natural environment and escape detection. For a sniper, it should also take away the recognizable human shape he adopts when he's hiding in a prone shooting position with his elbows up. You don't want your head and shoulders to ever give you away, and the ghillie suit can change up your contours so you're not as visible from afar.

Cam and concealment is as much about patience as it is about invisibility. And as snipers in training, we were often put through tests that seemed to challenge one aspect of our character when in fact a whole different thing was being tested and honed. You couldn't always predict the point from the outset. It's only later that it became clear.

Let me give you an example from our early cam and concealment exercises. On this concealment, four flags marked a rectangle 100 metres wide and 300 metres long. The field appeared to be barren, with just a few scraggly bushes, but nothing else. Our instructor was standing with binoculars in his hand next to a grey metal chair. "Okay, this is what we're going to do. I'm going to turn my back. You guys have seven minutes to go and hide. Then I'm going to sit in this chair and use my binos to try to spot you in the field."

A couple of guys were confused. "But there's hardly anywhere to hide."

"That's correct," the instructor said.

"And this field is mostly open," another guy said, "except for a few bushes."

"Congratulations. Your powers of observation are coming along nicely, Candidate," the instructor replied. Then he turned his back. "Okay. Go!" he announced, so off we ran. We headed for whatever cover we could find. Most people looking at that empty field—or box, as we called it—would not have seen anywhere to hide, but as snipers in training we were being taught why things were seen and how to avoid being one of them. Shape, surface, shadow, silhouette, spacing and movement—these were all things we learned to consider in concealment. We were learning to spot differences in elevation and use those as well. The difference between seen and not seen could be as little as a centimetre.

So there we were, hiding in the field. Seven minutes went by, then ten, then fifteen . . . nothing. Meanwhile, we were trying to remain in shooting positions, stock-still. Finally, after about twenty minutes, the instructor turned around, lifted his binoculars and sent walkers out into the box with radios. The walkers weren't allowed to just scope us out by sight. Instead, when the instructor spotted one of us, he'd give the walkers radioed instructions that led them to our various hiding spots. I could hear all of this going on, and even in the simulation exercise, I got that rush that comes when you know the enemy is just metres away and you could be discovered. For some people, it's all they can do to try to stay put because an alarm is going off in their heads that says, "Run! Run! Run!" And when you're a sniper hunkered down in a shitty hiding spot for over an hour, the whole point is to not move a muscle, because one twitch or flinch could give you away.

So, back in the field, we were still in hiding, waiting things out. When the walkers found you, they'd explain why you were caught. "You were seen because you didn't use enough depth. Remember that next time." Or, "You didn't wear enough camouflage, so your skin was visible even at a distance." Or, "We saw your combat boots." I learned then that black boots are a dead giveaway. You can be covered in camouflage, but if you forget to cover your boots, you're going to be seen. While being seen meant relatively little in training, in combat it meant something altogether more serious—it meant capture or death.

A few years after the sniper course, a platoon commander asked if I could do a tutorial for his platoon. I was happy to help, so I did this same field exercise with his soldiers. As a walker, I located this one kid, a machine gunner, hiding behind a bush. When I touched him to let him know he was found, he jumped up with his C9. "Fuck this, man!" he yelled. "I could have taken a shot a bunch of times by now and you would have been dead. This is bullshit!"

He was right, of course. He'd had ample time to shoot me. But that wasn't the exercise. Here was a soldier who was trigger-happy, who had one defensive tactic only—using his weapon. But a real sniper can lie in a shallow hole perfectly still, holding the urge to piss for hours on end. He can withstand the bad weather and physical discomfort and hunger without giving up and saying, "Fuck it, I'm outta here." Maybe this kid was an expert machine gunner, but he simply didn't have the right mentality to be a sniper.

When I was in sniper training, I loved learning skills that were not only about guns. My mentality right from the beginning was "Prepare for any eventuality," and I think that helped me be successful. There were so many lessons that were unexpected and hugely powerful, like the one about invisibility. A good sniper is invisible, but to master that skill you first have to understand why things are seen and how you get caught. Basically, we were taught how to think like the enemy, how to track targets, and the telltale signs to look out for that would tell us where even a master concealer was hiding. We were taught to watch out for movement above all else, but also to look out for colour, texture, contrasts and shadows that might betray a hidden enemy. I learned that when you are observing someone, you never look them in the eye, even if you're far enough away that he wouldn't be able to spot you. If you're eyeing someone, even from afar, at some point his sixth sense kicks in that tells him he's being watched.

Shooting is the coolest thing that snipers do, and it's what the world knows snipers for. But most of a sniper's time is spent not on shooting but on observation and information gathering, being the eyes and ears of the battle zone. If a vehicle drives by, a civilian might say, "A black car passed by at 12:33 p.m." But a sniper would be expected to observe more deeply. Did it have a dent in the bumper? What was the licence plate? Who was the driver? Were there passengers? This particular skill came in very handy later on when I was in Kabul. It wasn't good enough there to say, "I saw a yellow-and-white Toyota Tercel on the road." There were hundreds of yellow-and-white Toyota Tercels. We were trained to spot minute details that would identify a specific car, its driver and its passengers. And we learned to do that in a matter of seconds.

To train for this, in sniper school we often did an exercise called the KIMS—or Keep in Mind—game. Ten items would be put on a table and we'd have sixty seconds to look at them all and try to remember as much about them as we could. For example, a bunch of weapons-cleaning items like bore rags, lubricant cleaners and other things would be placed out for observation, then taken away after one minute.

Then our instructors would quiz us. "What colour were the bore rags? Were they two-by-two or bigger? Were they used or brand new? How many were stacked on top of each other? How many piles were there? What brand was the cleaner? How big was the jar? There was a watch on the table: what time did it say?"

We would have only a couple of minutes to write down our answers. As observers, it didn't take us long to discover just how fallible memory can be. We learned a key phrase—"ATB," which stood for "appears to be." If as a witness you started with a definitive statement—"There were"—there was no room later for further remembrances or clarifications. We learned to report this way: "It *appears to be* there were ten stacks of rags." This gave you a little bit of wiggle room and allowed the listener to hear the difference between a hard fact (the rags were red) and an educated or deductive guess (there appeared to be ten stacks).

As we got better, the game got bigger, moving from objects on a table to objects in a room, then to a field with objects hidden throughout it. We'd observe the field from various angles, and the objects could be anywhere from ten to three hundred metres away. We were trained to use our eyes first, then our binos, and last, our spotting scopes. We'd scan right to left, rather than left to right, because we scan more slowly when we do it the opposite way we read. Again, we looked for shape, shadow, contrast—and anything else that looked out of place. We got so addicted to these exercises that we started doing this to each other as a joke when we weren't even in class. A buddy would walk into a room and I'd close the door behind him and ask, "What was in the hallway?"

"What?"

"KIMS game. Fast. What did you see?"

"Oh! Uh . . . Red fire extinguisher, halfway up the far wall. A flyer for the pub next door that said 'Wing Night Wednesday.' Fluorescent lights overhead, one bulb out. Uh, grey carpet, worn right at the door with a piece of old gum stuck close to the threshold." We got sharper and sharper the more we played.

This skill was amazingly transferable once we were on mission. And one day, only a few weeks into our sniper course, that reality suddenly got a whole lot closer.

8

THE WAR ON TERROR BEGINS

O N T H E morning of September 11, 2001, I was taking in a lecture on ballistics. A few minutes after the class started, the duty sergeant burst into the room with an urgent message. "Someone just flew a plane into the World Trade Center!"

The instructor teaching the class was annoyed. "Thanks so much for the newscast, but we've got a class to teach here." The duty sergeant stared at us in disbelief, but we all figured the plane must have been a little Cessna or a prop-engine and that the whole thing had been an accident—maybe the pilot was some drunken fool. It sure wasn't an emergency, and we were not thrilled our class had been interrupted.

Without another word, the duty sergeant left the room. About twenty minutes later, he burst back in, this time with even more urgency in his voice. "A *second* plane just flew into the World Trade Center! This is not an accident. This is an attack on the United States!"

Our instructor changed his tune. "Okay, let's go see what's happening. Class dismissed."

We went down the hallway to the duty station, which served as the welcome centre for guests arriving on the base. There was a television tuned to one of the news channels. As soon as we walked into the room, the live shot of the first tower collapsing stopped us in our tracks. It looked like a Hollywood movie. How could this possibly be real? We stood watching, jaws agape.

"It's a hijacking," someone said. "This was done on purpose. Twice."

In a matter of minutes, the world had changed. The freedom of North Americans was suddenly in jeopardy. There was a feeling in the room like this was "game on," and in my head I could almost hear the bugle call just before a horse race. Over the past years, I had sometimes considered leaving the army and moving into the police force, but at that moment, something in me switched. Watching that footage of those buildings collapse in New York, I knew the idea of leaving would never cross my mind again.

Within minutes, our military went on high alert. All our bases, right across the country, went into lockdown. Gates were closed, and anyone wanting in had to provide full identification, a contact on the inside and a clear reason for visiting the base. The same applied for leaving the base: you had to present full ID and a reason for leaving.

That day, we were issued orders to pack up our gear with three days' worth of supplies and be ready for deployment within twenty-four hours. The base went from calm and curriculum-focused to frenetic and chaotic. Some guys were not used to the stress level, and it was starting to show. The usual speed limit on the base was 40 kilometres per hour, but guys now whipped around at close to a hundred. The chaos was so widespread that I almost got run over by one of the mechanics. I'll never forget the guy's expression of wide-eyed shock as he zoomed past me in his old Ford pickup. One had to wonder: was national security hinging on this mechanic?

On the night of September 11, we slept in our platoon areas at our unit headquarters. It felt like we were a football team that for some kind of exercise was spending the night not in our hotel but on the locker room floor. One of the soldiers had *Band of Brothers*, the TV miniseries about an American regiment that fought in World War II. As we cleaned our weapons and packed and repacked our rucksacks, we watched the show. Everybody was keyed up. Word was circulating that the attacks in the States might be related to Muslim extremists.

While this was going on, I had serious concerns that I was going to miss out on the rest of my sniper training course. While I certainly wanted to be thrown into the middle of the action, I also wanted to do so as a trained sniper. Fortunately—or unfortunately, depending on your point of view—Canada didn't quite have the military capability and resources to react on a world scale on such short notice. We knew that we were likely going to be involved in this "war on terror" at some point. The question was: when?

For me, this meant I still had some training time. It was decided that the sniper course would continue—business as usual for the foreseeable future. I was both relieved and excited on the day that sniper training resumed. There was just one problem: Joint Task Force 2, an elite unit of the Canadian Special Operations Forces, had taken over most of our training grounds. Those grounds were now being used to practise air strikes using CF-18s. We were forced to train elsewhere. Our course instructor got creative and we moved to the military's Connaught Range and Primary Training Centre, just outside of Ottawa, where we continued our field firing drills. That was essential, because to complete the course, we had to do live-fire exercises to a range of 900 metres. The area had to have shrubbery, rocks and some geographical features. Bullets ricocheted in all directions, so a vast tract of land was the only way such drills could be done safely. Once we finished our field firing drills in the new field, we were moved yet again, back to our old infantry battle school in Meaford, Ontario.

Even though we were senior soldiers now, that drive up the hill to

Meaford still gave us all that sinking feeling just like when we were first on our way there as recruits. The training centre in Meaford was filled with raw recruits doing their basic infantry training, so when all of us snipers in training showed up, we were the rock stars on the base.

While we were at Meaford, our skills were honed in the art of stalking, one of the most important and hardest skills to master for any field soldier but especially for snipers. All of a sniper's skills come together in this exercise where the sniper has to use stealth to get from one end of a field (called the box) to the other. The objective was to get no closer than 100 metres and no farther than 300 metres from the spotters without being seen. The spotters, trained snipers themselves, were set up on chairs on the edge of the box and decked out in binoculars. If you made it into range without getting spotted, you could then prepare your shooting position and take your shot with a blank round. At the end, you had to extract yourself without being detected.

The whole exercise involved crawling on our hands, knees and belly, inching along like worms, changing our camouflage as we went over a terrain that stretched for two kilometres—all while not being spotted. Surprisingly enough, most soldiers don't find it a fun pastime to crawl for two kilometres. At the best of times, stalking is tough, but in the fall, when all the leaves are on the ground, it's an extra challenge. And it's not just your own weight you're moving. You've got a weapon with you—your rifle—which you have to drag along in something called a drag bag. Move too slowly, and you'll never make it all the way on time; move too fast and you'll be caught. Stealth was essential, and pacing was something you learned from practice.

There's nothing quite like the feeling of hiding out in a hollow or behind a bush and seeing the walker get closer and closer. Sometimes the walker would be right on top of you. He'd be five steps away, four, three. *He* could see you just fine, but as long as the observer didn't spot you from a distance, you were safe, still in the game.

All through sniper training, we were losing guys who didn't make it through the various tests. But when it came to the stalking test, it was a bloodbath. Soldiers were allowed to fail a couple of stalks, but if they failed four in a row, they were immediately disqualified, with no chance of a retake. It was so difficult that seven guys in the course ended up failing. By the time we got through stalking, there were only three of us left—Ben, Dave and me.

Next, we moved on to long-range field firing. Targets were presented, but you didn't know how far away they were. You had to look through your scope, assess the distance, aim and take your shot, all in a matter of minutes. For this drill, a spotter watched the target and gave you directions. The spotter could usually tell if you hit your target by watching the bullet swirl through the air, something you would not be able to see while shooting. If you didn't hit the target, he'd tell you how to adjust for your next shot. But if the spotter's directions were off, it could mess you up.

We practised firing over and over, and eventually, it was time for the long-range field firing test. The first time I did it, I was doing great, up to about 600 metres. The targets from 600 metres to 900 metres were a challenge. My spotter was having a hard time seeing if my bullets were hitting the targets, so as the distances were getting longer, I was moving more and more off target. Eventually, I was missing the targets altogether. Luckily, I had three chances to pass the test. That first one was a fail. I failed the second time as well because, for some reason, my spotter and I weren't jibing, and I was off my mark yet again.

I had only one more chance. To say I was nervous about this last attempt is an understatement. If I failed this one test, I was out of sniper training and my dream of becoming a sniper was over. Meanwhile,

Dave and Ben were almost as spooked as I was. When I asked if either wanted to be my spotter for the final test, they said, "Jody, man, we don't want the responsibility if you fail. We all know what that means."

The pressure was on. In the end, Ben agreed to be my spotter. To pass, I needed to hit sixteen out of twenty targets. Once I got up to the longer distances—like 700 metres or 800 metres—I just needed to hit the target somewhere, anywhere at all. It didn't have to be a bull's-eye shot. I was firing away and actually shooting fairly well with Ben's spotting help. But as I approached the end of the round, the last target was up and I had fifteen hits. It was do or die. All I needed was to make this last shot, just one more shot. I aimed. I pulled the trigger. "Did I hit it?" I asked.

Ben was quiet for moment. "Um. Not sure, Jody."

It wasn't a bull's-eye—that much was clear. In fact, there were no clear signs of a hit. But when we got up close, Ben noticed a small nick at the very top of the target.

"Yes! Yes! You hit it!" Ben said. My bullet had grazed the top of the target just enough to qualify for a hit, and with that, I had passed the field firing test and could remain in the course.

Next, I had to pass the final training exercise, what we called FTX. Dave, Ben and I, the last men standing, were given the weekend to prepare for the most important test of our lives. We packed and re-packed our rucksacks, which is what soldiers do when they're on edge. At 4 a.m. the following Monday, we deployed for our four-day sniper mission, a test of all of the skills we had learned throughout the course.

Dave and I were partners. The whole thing was hell. We didn't sleep more than about four hours in four days. It rained most of the time and we even had to deal with sleet one day. We did great at observing and reporting activities on a target location. This was a scenario where our intelligence-gathering led to shooting on the "enemy" target before they could launch a mission. We did have some struggles shooting a reactive target that would set off an explosion; we didn't manage to set it off. Lucky for us, that wasn't enough of a reason for us to not pass. Also, we did really well at cam and concealment. We were so good at tactical movement that the instructors called a pause in the exercise because they had no idea where in the training area we were, even though Dave had some misgivings about my techniques. When you're observing a target in the prone position, you can't just stand up, wander off and take a piss. The tactical solution is to roll as far away from your sniper partner as you can and pee lying down. But because you're usually concealed in a low spot, there are times when, despite your best diversionary tactics, the trickle rolls right back to your partner. Unfortunately, I have been cursed with a small bladder and I am very careful to always stay well hydrated, so after about the fifth or sixth time of me doing this to Dave, he finally cracked. "What the fuck, Mitic?" he complained. "If you don't stop that, they're going to find us by the smell of your piss!"

The good news: Dave was wrong. Piss or no piss, they never did find us, and after four days, end of exercise was called. At long last, we could call ourselves snipers.

9

MARRIED TO THE ARMY

I HAD NO idea how much passing the sniper course would change how I was perceived by my old company.

I returned to my Bravo Company, 5 Platoon (which is where I was posted after battle school) in December of 2001. Because it was close to Christmas, a lot of soldiers had returned home for the holidays, so the base was fairly empty. And since I lived close to Petawawa, I didn't take much time off. One day, I was sitting in the company office, which is usually reserved for people with higher rankings than mine, but since most of the base was deserted, I figured I could get away with hanging out there and I might actually see a few people. Usually, as a corporal, I stayed in the platoon area and visited the offices only when I was directly invited.

I walked into the office and the atmosphere was surprisingly welcoming. Sergeants and officers suddenly treated me differently, as if I had moved up a rank. They no longer greeted me with doubt cloaked in formality: "Hello, Corporal Mitic." Now it was more like "Hey Jody! How are you?"

A handful of senior staff were shooting the breeze and I grabbed a seat alongside them. They were discussing how they needed a couple of lower-ranking guys to do some grunt work. It wasn't anything demeaning, just something nobody wanted to do, something best completed by a couple of privates and a corporal. Since it was the holidays and the place was almost deserted, the pickings were pretty slim.

I was waiting for them to put the task on me. Sure enough, a fairly new officer piped up. "What about Mitic? He's a corporal and he's sitting right here. Why can't he do it?"

Everybody stared at her as if she had just made a major mistake.

"Look," I said, "I know you're having a hard time finding someone to do the job. I'll take care of it."

One of the sergeants said, "Are you sure? You don't have to if you don't want to."

"You know what, I'm kind of bored anyway," I said. "I'll go grab a couple of guys from the maintenance area. We'll get it done."

As I left those offices and set out to get the job done, I realized that I might still be Corporal Jody Mitic in name, but sniper training had just opened up a whole new world to me. It was flattering to be treated as an equal of the officers in the room, even though they all outranked me.

•

Shortly after New Year's, we held our annual winter training exercises. I learned that I was going to be a section 2IC, or second-in-command, for my group's training drills. Considering I had no formal leadership training, this was a pretty big responsibility. The first part of the exercise was a recce mission to stake out a target that would later be attacked. I was a little surprised when the higher-ups said, "Mitic, grab a couple of people and recce this site for us. Then let us know your findings."

I took three soldiers and we did a recce of an area that was being occupied by a pretend enemy force. We did it in the snow in the middle of the day, came back and shared our intelligence. The next day, after the recce, I was talking to the soldiers who were playing the enemy force.

"What? When did you recce us?" one of them asked me.

"Yesterday," I said. "Around noon. You didn't notice our tracks in the snow?"

"No. We had no idea. Good recce!"

In most cases, if you navigate for the recce team that stakes out a target, you also navigate for the platoon in the subsequent attack. That's SOP—standard operating procedure. But when it was time to lead our platoon on the mock attack, one of the master corporals in our section— a guy known for questionable decisions and for his outstanding ability to get lost—stood up and said, "Actually, I'm going to lead this mission." I was stunned. This guy hadn't been part of the recce team that scouted out the position, so how was he going to know where to go?

"Mitic, you will be in charge of left flank security," I was told. It was bad enough that someone else was going to navigate for the platoon after I had done all the recce work, but it was adding salt to the wound that I was put on left flank instead of being with the main assault group. Normally, if someone was leading other than the head of the recce mission, at least the new navigator would have the recce leader by his side so he could help guide the group forward.

When I'd done the recce the day before, my fellow soldier Crystal had been on the team. She was now paired with me on left flank.

"Does this make sense to you?" she asked.

"Not really," I said.

As we set out, the problems became apparent right away.

"Crystal," I whispered once we were out in the field, "do you recognize this area?"

"No, I don't," she replied.

"That's because we never came this way yesterday," I said. "And this isn't the route we planned for the attack."

Crystal and I were so far back in the group it would have been impossible for us to alert the leaders that they were totally off track. We were not equipped with radios, so we had no way to communicate with the platoon commander. We were walking in the wrong direction, and not just a little bit—*kilometres* in the wrong direction, in the snow, in the dark.

About thirty minutes later, we did a long halt, where everybody stopped and gathered in a circle. The leadership huddled in the middle to discuss the next move. Crystal and I were on the sidelines and couldn't hear what was said.

Still, I had a hunch what was going down. I turned to Crystal and said, "Watch this."

Right on cue, I heard a crunching of footsteps through the snow and the master corporal called out.

"Hey Mitic! Mitic, buddy. Come on over here."

I went over to the huddle to confer with the leadership group. "Hey guys, what's going on?" I was playing dumb.

"Where are we?" the master corporal asked.

On the ground in front of the group was a map of the area. "This is where we are right now," I said, pointing to a spot way off course. "And *this* is where we want to be," I added, pointing out our intended destination on the other side of the map.

"So, um . . . How about if Mitic helps with the final approach to the attack area," the master corporal suggested.

"Yeah, of course. No problem." I tried to hide my I-told-you-so smile. "Just one question. Didn't you see the tracks in the snow from yesterday? Those were my tracks. Why didn't you just follow those?"

"Oh, we didn't realize those were yours," the master corporal said. "I guess we got a little turned around."

And with that, I took over the navigation role I should have had from the beginning. I would navigate the platoon out to the site and then the master corporal would take over when the attack phase started.

I got us back on the position. But when it came time for the master corporal to break out his blue glow stick, which was the signal for us to deploy troops to their spots for the attack, he had a problem. "Oh shit, oh shit," he kept repeating.

"So what's the matter?" I asked dryly.

"Oh nothing," he said. But it was clear what had happened. He was checking his pockets, his rucksack—everywhere—but he couldn't find the glow stick. "Why don't you go up and alert the platoon commander that we're all set," he said.

So off I went to the platoon commander. As soon as she saw me, she asked, "What happened to the glow-stick plan?"

"I don't know," I responded. "But here's your position to launch the attack."

As I stood there, I looked back over at the master corporal, who was waving a penlight at us. The platoon commander gave me a questioning look, which I avoided while grinning.

The whole episode reminded me that sometimes in the army ranks, those in charge of missions and exercises aren't necessarily the best qualified. There's always 10 percent of soldiers at every level and rank who will leave you wondering how they ever completed basic training and managed to make their way up the chain of command.

Not long after the winter exercises, a massive reorganization of companies got under way. This is a fairly common practice in the Armed Forces, with troops shifted around every couple of years. Some of the guys from Bravo Company could move over to Alpha Company, which might send some of their guys over to Foxtrot Company, and so on. At the same time, the unit kept a core base of people in each company, to maintain some stability. I was put into the sniper section with my colleague Dave.

This was exactly what I was hoping for, since my ultimate goal was to be deployed overseas as a sniper in the war on terror. There is a certain amount of "cool guy" factor that goes along with officially being part of the sniper section. Suddenly my input mattered when it came to strategic decisions, and senior staff started to seek out my counsel. Commanders who want a sniper team treat snipers differently. And the snipers don't actually take orders from the company commander; snipers are there in roles of support, not subservience. Commanders can make suggestions to the team, but ultimately, the team tells the commander what their capabilities are. If a company commander says the plan is to attack a village, the snipers' job is to come up with the best plan to support the operation of that mission. And as a sniper, you have more "operational freedom," which puts you in control of a lot of your decisions.

•

Shortly after joining the sniper section, I competed in something called CFSAC, the Canadian Forces Small Arms Concentration. This is a series of shooting competitions held annually at the Connaught Range, where I had done some of my sniper training. We kept our marksman skills sharp by shooting thousands and thousands of practice rounds in the spring and summer of 2002. We used all kinds of firearms—pistols, assault rifles, machine guns. Snipers tend to shoot at least twice a month, at least a hundred rounds each time. People don't often realize how physically demanding shooting is. But we prepared as much as we could for the competition, and the extra practice was welcomed.

At the CFSAC competition, our four-person sniper team got the best aggregate score, and I came away with the top tyro award for best new shooter ("tyro" meaning novice in army speak). We came back to Petawawa feeling pretty good about ourselves and our shooting ability.

Later that year, I was sent to Gagetown, New Brunswick, for a couple of events at the military base. First, along with other snipers in training, I did a trial for a new rifle—a .338 Lapua magnum to replace the .308 one. We were given ten different brands to try out, and we were asked for our feedback on which ones we liked and which ones we didn't. These rifles had adjustable scopes and were totally different from the ones we normally used. Our favourite was a gun called the Timberwolf, made by a Canadian company in Winnipeg.

One of the highlights of that trip was meeting Rob Furlong, who was a new legend in the sniper community. He had just returned home from Afghanistan, where, during Operation Anaconda, he set the world record for the farthest sniper kill using a .50-calibre sniper rifle called the Tac-50. Furlong had a confirmed sniper kill at a distance of 2430 metres. Ironically, a few years later, Furlong's record would be broken by a British soldier using the .338 magnum that we were then testing in New Brunswick.

A couple of months later, I competed in the International Sniper Competition, at Fort Benning, Georgia. This event is highly regarded in the community and brings together some of the best snipers in the world. That year was an especially significant one, because the war in Afghanistan was escalating and many snipers at the competition had a lot of recent operational experience. I was keen to listen to their stories and get tips from experienced people in the field. It was like any other networking conference in the high-tech or marketing world, except our group was a bunch of highly trained gunmen.

•

Things were fairly quiet for me after I returned home from that trip. I had just purchased my first home and decided to move off the base for the first time. My house was in a tiny town called Chalk River, situated between the base and the town of Deep River. The population of Chalk River was about five hundred people, and at least half of them were military.

JODY MITIC

The house was spacious enough for me, but it would soon become a place for two. I had been dating a woman for a couple of years. She and I had met on St. Patrick's Day in 2001 and we had been a fairly steady item ever since. A few weeks after I bought my house, she moved in. She was very focused on one goal—getting married and having four kids by the time she was twenty-five. We talked about this, of course. I expressed that I was focused on my military career and that I wasn't sure getting married and having a few kids was on my short-term radar.

Nonetheless, she stayed with me, even though there wasn't much for her to do in a tiny town like Chalk River. She was going to school, but even when she was finished, the job opportunities in this area were going to be extremely limited. And if I was deployed on a mission overseas, what would she do? I had a sinking feeling that me and this town wouldn't be good enough for her in the long term.

One day, she wanted me to go on a drive with her out to a nearby lake. "Do we really have to?" I asked. I had no interest in heading outside on a cold and windy day.

"Yes, we do," she said.

We got in the car and drove to the lake. Then we walked down to the shore. The weather was unpleasant, which prompted me to ask, "What are we doing here?"

She didn't have an answer for me, and I could tell that something was going on with her. We got back into the car and had an awkward drive home.

When we arrived, I went to the bedroom to change. Before I could even get dressed, she pulled me out to the living room. She sat me on the couch and said, "Will you marry me?"

It took a few moments for that question to sink in. I was absolutely floored that not only had my girlfriend just proposed to me, she'd done so while I was buck-naked!

Suddenly the trip to the lake made a whole lot of sense. She had wanted to ask me there but got too nervous when the moment arrived. Apparently she had no hesitation popping the question while I was in the buff in the living room, though.

I said to her, "Before we get married, I have a few conditions. I don't want us carrying any debt, so I want to get some things paid off first. Also, I think we need to figure out our career paths. I don't want your whole life to revolve around my schedule with the army."

She was okay with these conditions, so we had a loose engagement, until the time when I would buy her a ring and propose more formally. But then I had a great idea. "Instead of an engagement ring," I said, "why don't I get you something way cooler, like a motorcycle or a personalized gun?"

"I don't want a fucking gun," she said. "I want a wedding ring!"

Oh well. We could have added a whole new meaning to "shotgun wedding."

We were cruising along in our relationship into the spring of 2003. We still hadn't set a wedding date, but there was another date on the calendar that was looming even larger. The Canadian government was looking to increase its presence in Afghanistan and word was that a new deployment would happen shortly. When the orders for my deployment came through, I suggested to my girlfriend that maybe she should consider going back to Brampton to live with her family for six months instead of being so isolated in Chalk River.

"No," she said. "I'll wait for you in our home." Since we were engaged, she felt like this was where her life was.

But neither of us knew then that I would come back from my first tour in Afghanistan a changed man. What we both would come to learn is that I couldn't marry her, because in my heart I was already married—to the army.

AFGHANISTAN

23 July 2003.

HOT. HOT. HOT. And dusty.
Thats it in a nutshell. Add
windy too. The 120 days of wind
is only half over. I think.
Everything you have seen on T.V.
and the movies is true. This
place is wrecked. The people
live in squaller at best.
But they are all trying to
get on with it. At a slow pace
anyway. They never hurry because
they know it will get done when
it is done. And they love to
stare. Friendly though.
Say hi to everyone and
take care. Love JODY

Printed By: Karam Poster House LHR. Tel: 7248772

Cpl Mitic 461
Op Athena
HQ + Sig Rover Trp.
Camp Warehouse
PO Box 5006 Stn Forces
Belleville ON
K8N 5W6

Post Card

2003 -08- 01

CANADIAN FORCES MAIL
COURRIER DES FORCES CANADIENNES

Hemi Mitic
8 Lisa St #1608
Brampton ON Can
L6T 4S6

Made In Pakistan

PART
3

The highest obligation and privilege of citizenship is that of bearing arms for one's country.

—General George S. Patton Jr.

10

INTO AFGHANISTAN: IMPROVISE, ADAPT, OVERCOME

HE AMERICANS launched their attack on Iraq in the spring of 2003. At the time, I was at CFB Wainwright, Alberta, doing more training. A group of other soldiers and I gathered around the TV, watching the U.S. assault as it was broadcast live around the globe. We were all thinking the same thing: it's only a matter of time.

As it turned out, Canada declined to be involved with that mission in Iraq, but our government decided to increase its presence in Afghanistan. The first set of new troops to deploy was 3rd Battalion, Royal Canadian Regiment, or 3 RCR, categorized as a light infantry battalion. There was quite a rivalry between 3 RCR and my 1st Battalion, or 1 RCR, which was mechanized infantry. When I asked if 3 RCR needed snipers, I was told, "Sorry, we aren't going to need you in that role. We have enough snipers of our own."

That was a real punch in the gut, but I wasn't going to let it stop me from being deployed to Afghanistan. I'd waited long enough. So when the role of a driver and bodyguard came up, I inquired. What they needed were a couple of infantry guys—guys with combat arms experience—who could drive vehicles and get key personnel around Kabul safely. It would be a far cry from being deployed as a sniper, but at least it was something.

Before I took the position, I asked one more time: "Is there any way I can be a sniper?"

"No. There is zero chance," the deployment officer said. "And this driver role is basically one of the last spots available. So do you want to go over or not?"

"Okay, I'll go," I said. My buddy Gord took the other driver post, so at least we'd be together.

The very next day, a call went out for two more snipers. Gord and I quickly went to the deployment officer.

"Those roles are fuckin' ours!" we said.

"Sorry," the deployment officer answered, probably because he didn't want to do the paperwork. "You've already accepted your roles as drivers. You can't change courses now. Besides, we've already filled those sniper spots."

We were hugely disappointed, but the decision was beyond our control. We made the best of it and prepared for our tour in Afghanistan.

We arrived in Kabul in June of 2003 and quickly got the lay of the land. There were two Canadian camps set up in the area. The main one was Camp Julien, on the grounds of the old king and queen's palace. The other was a smaller base, Camp Warehouse, which was out of the city centre, right next to the airport. That's where I was stationed, while Gord was sent to TV Tower Hill, at the top of a mountain in the middle of Kabul. His role was to keep this isolated post, which was used as a communications relay station, safe from ambush.

Meanwhile, I was placed in the rover troop inside Camp Warehouse, which meant I was both driver and security for anyone who required it while moving around Kabul. I often escorted liaison officers into the city for meetings they had with the Afghan army and police. Other times, I took officers to foreign embassies. My instructions were received the day of the drive: "Mitic, today you're taking the colonel to the Turkish embassy."

After orders were issued, I'd sit through a briefing where we would investigate security threats, the weather and any other factors that could have an impact on the driving route. We travelled in two vehicles, one lead vehicle and one secondary. Each would have a driver and co-driver, as well as passengers. We always travelled wearing our full military uniforms. We were easy to identify as members of the Canadian Armed Forces, so we had to be extra cautious in public spaces. A handful of Canadian soldiers were assigned work in the city in civilian clothes, but those were mainly intelligence operatives doing reconnaissance work.

I quickly learned the easy routes into the city, but I have to admit, getting the hang of Kabul wasn't easy. I'm notorious for being bad at urban navigation. Put me out in a forest without a compass and I'll be fine, but if you stick me downtown with a ton of buildings, I have major problems getting my bearings. My brother always makes fun of me. "Jody," he'll say when we're driving around Toronto, "you're a highly skilled sniper with years of navigation training. How come you can't go downtown without getting lost?"

The side streets in Kabul were an absolute shit show—in more ways than one. The narrow roads were not paved and were often knee-deep in mud. And because Kabul lacked a sophisticated sewage system, raw sewage leaked out into the streets in a potent and identifiable blend of urine, feces and other muck. There were sheep and goats in the streets, along with bikes, trucks and motorcycles. People were even driving random pieces of construction equipment. There were people pulling carts. There were people pushing carts. There were herds of camels. Also, Afghans are never in a hurry . . . unless they're behind the wheel of a vehicle, in which case it's full speed ahead. There were intersections where no one really stopped, and the roads ranged from horse tracks that were about as pitted as the surface of the moon to wide boulevards that were runway smooth.

It would drive me nuts when my fellow drivers would speed through an area where there were kids running around and playing. I would get on my radio. "Slow the fuck down! These kids aren't raised like the ones back in Canada. They're not looking both ways before they cross the street. Hit a kid and I will make sure you're charged and go to fucking jail."

Our vehicles for this mission were Iltis, which were a lot like small jeeps. They were great for traversing all terrains because they were so light. The doors were made of flimsy vinyl and the windshield of laminated safety glass. The downside was these vehicles weren't tremendously safe, which I suppose accounts for why security was needed to begin with.

One day, we were sent on a mission with two Iltis vehicles driving together. I drove with a single passenger, and the other car had two passengers, one of whom was a lieutenant who also happened to be an attractive blonde. We made it into the city but lost our way in the narrow streets. We ended up near a big, busy public market. Suddenly the shoppers noticed the lieutenant, who was in full uniform. They started reaching out towards her, pointing at her blond hair and blue eyes. They were desperate for a better glimpse and were banging on the windows hard enough to make us worry they would break. We peeled away from the crowd just in time, but that experience left a bad taste in the mouths of some of our senior staff, who now saw the dangers of driving around in such primitive vehicles.

The Iltis jeeps were not designed to withstand idle curiosity, never mind an attack. This fact became starkly apparent when three 3 RCR guys were driving an Iltis and hit a land mine. Two of them—Sergeant Robert Short and Corporal Rob Beerenfenger—died immediately, and the driver, T.J. Stirling, a friend of mine, survived though he was injured. After the incident, T.J. was brought to the hospital at Camp Warehouse, and me and another one of the guys from the regiment went to see him. This was the first time I'd seen one of our guys hit by a land mine. In fact, it was the first time I'd seen a casualty at all.

T.J. was pretty banged up. A couple of his teeth were broken and he may have had a broken jaw. He had lacerations all over. There's always a particular odour in hospitals around people who have suffered traumatic injuries. I remember smelling that odour, like blood, or maybe just what I thought blood smelled like. T.J. was on a stretcher with big wheels. We'd used this kind of stretcher before in training. To me, it was a kind of prop, this thing we used for simulations. But this was not a simulation. This was the real thing.

T.J. was still in shock. It had taken a few hours for him to be extracted from the scene of the explosion. "Shorty and Beerenfenger are gone," he said.

"Yeah, man," we replied. "We heard."

"I need a smoke, man. I need a smoke," T.J. said. The doctors and nurses wouldn't allow it, but as soon as they were out of the vicinity, we lit a cigarette for T.J. and gave him a couple of drags.

"Ahhhh. That's way better. Thanks."

We stayed and chatted with T.J. about inconsequential things, trying to keep a fellow Royal in a good state of mind. For me personally, I was learning from what was happening, facing the reality that when things go wrong you have to get that smell in your nostrils and look those sights right in the eye. Sadly, a few years later, T.J. ended up taking his own life. I was a pall bearer at his funeral, and as I carried his coffin, I wondered if he'd carried guilt for being the lone survivor in that accident.

After this tragic event, new vehicles were dispatched for our use—durable Nissan mini-SUVs. These cars had four-cylinder diesel engines and could handle the crappy and muddy road conditions in Kabul without getting stuck. And they came with air-conditioning, which was a much-appreciated feature in the hot weather. The Nissan also had an interior air-filter system, which helped block out the horrendous stench that hung in the Kabul air.

From sunrise to sunset, Kabul was a bustling city, but outside of those hours it was eerily quiet. The place was not only jammed with other vehicles, it was filled with hundreds of civilians walking the streets, many of whom were beggars in a desperate state. As part of our pre-mission briefings, we were explicitly ordered to avoid giving handouts to beggars and children.

"You need to understand this," I remember being told. "You create a security concern when you have large groups of kids gathered outside your vehicle or around your military gates looking for spare change. You don't want them to be targeted if you happen to be attacked, and you don't want to set the precedent that soldiers are there to give handouts. That's not our mission. There are times when you're going to see things that are pretty ugly, but that's Afghanistan. Remember that."

One time, I was driving down the road in Kabul when I noticed the cars ahead of me swerving to avoid an obstacle smack-dab in the middle of the road. As I approached, I saw that the obstacle was a woman. She was wearing a white burka, and wrapped in a blanket she held in her arms a tiny newborn baby. She was distraught and begging for money in the middle of the street as cars whizzed past, narrowly missing her. As we drove closer, I got a good look at her and her infant. As she held out the child, the reason for her despair became apparent.

The newborn's mouth was ringed black. The baby looked completely lifeless. Cars honked and swerved around this mother, and not knowing what to do, I did the same. I didn't even stop to throw any change her way. To this day, it bothers me that I didn't do something. As the commander of the convoy, I had the authority to address situations like this one. I could have stopped, put her in the car and checked to see if the baby was alive. If it was, I could have rushed her to the hospital. But I drove away.

This sort of thing was common all over Kabul. With each passing day, I grew more desensitized to the poverty and misery that so many of the Afghan people were suffering. One day, I saw this little boy who had a serious birth defect. His elbows were inverted, which made him look like his arms were almost upside down. He had tiny hands that looked like they were not functional at all. This boy came over to me and wrapped his arms around my legs, giving me a big hug. As he did this, he looked up at me with big puppy-dog eyes. "Please, please, please," he said in broken English, over and over again. I'd trained as a soldier and a sniper for years. I'd learned to put my emotions aside and to concentrate on actions and orders. But in that moment, it was almost impossible not to feel an urgent tug at my heart.

Going against every instinct I felt, I gently pulled the boy off me. "I'm sorry," I said. "I can't give you money."

"Please, please, please."

"I'm sorry," I said, pushing his deformed arms away. Standing behind him was an older child who looked to be his brother. The older boy grabbed his little brother and led him to another soldier nearby.

"Please, please, please," I heard as I kept walking, quickly heading to camp.

Some beggars and panhandlers came up with creative ways to get money from NATO soldiers. One day, a Canadian Forces light armoured vehicle hit a Toyota Tercel that was ripping around the roads at about a hundred kilometres per hour while filled floor to roof with passengers. Soon after, one of the men in the car went to the Canadian Forces asking for compensation for his injuries. He said his neck was injured, but more critically, his wife had suffered two broken legs in the accident. He wanted a few thousand dollars to cover medical bills and to compensate for the fact that someone had to look after the kids now that his wife was incapacitated.

The story sounded good—at first. But when our military officers studied photos of the accident scene, they noticed something suspicious.

"This is your wife right here, correct?" they asked the man.

"Yes," he replied.

"Well," they said, proffering some other shots, "here she is after the accident walking away from the scene—on two unbroken legs."

As it turned out, the man had gone home after the accident and broken his wife's legs himself, thinking he could pin her injuries on the accident and be awarded damages. We arrested him and turned him over to the Afghan authorities. Who knows if he was ever charged or saw jail time. Sadly, things like this were fairly common in Kabul.

When I communicated with my friends and family back home, I didn't share too many stories like these. I kept them mostly to myself and focused more on hearing news from home instead. I noticed, too, that sometimes when I did bring up some of the harder things I'd witnessed, the subject would get changed pretty quickly.

After about three months in Kabul, I had a much-needed three-week getaway in New Zealand with my girlfriend. We toured the countryside, stayed in beautiful hostels and marvelled at the scenery. The worst danger we encountered was the sheep, which would sometimes amble onto the roadway.

"Sheep!" my girlfriend would yell out, grabbing my arm in panic.

"Don't worry," I'd say, laughing. "I saw them coming long ago."

How could I tell her I'd avoided much worse things on the roads in Kabul?

Believe it or not, even though I enjoyed those three weeks away, I was glad to get back to my post. And I think some of the officers were happy to see me back, too. I would often overhear senior officers asking, "Hey, can Mitic and his team take us to the embassy today?" I had a reputation as a hard-ass who would make sure passengers got in and out of Kabul safely.

In fact, I got so good at my job as a driver and bodyguard that my chain of command refused to let me serve as a sniper for a few weeks when the opportunity arose. I was pretty disappointed, because I always felt that a bad day with the sniper section was still going to be better than the best day as a driver. The words of Uncle Billy echoed in my mind. I managed to put a smile on my face and soldier on. I was hitting the gym twice a day and I probably put on about twenty pounds of lean muscle during the tour. By the end of it, I could bench-press about 315 pounds. Some of the guys jokingly referred to me as the Joint Task Force member of the rover troop, but I was never offended. "Look," I'd answer. "I don't get behind the wheel like it's a Sunday drive. I drive like we're on a mission because we *are*."

•

Although we were much safer once we were driving the mini-SUV Nissans, we had major problems with our weapons. We'd been issued C7 rifles to carry with us, but C7s are about a metre long, which makes them very awkward to manoeuvre inside a vehicle. We were forced to put them in the back seat because the front was filled with radios, headsets and a GPS system that allowed the base to track our every move. I didn't like the fact that we couldn't easily access our weapons, so I started making some noise to the higher-ups.

I wanted a C8 rifle, which was smaller than its C7 counterpart, and

I wanted each driver issued a pistol. The problem was that the chain of command viewed the C8 and pistols as weapons for soldiers classified as officers and above. They didn't see the need to give such firearms to corporals who were serving as drivers. Meanwhile, back at Camp Warehouse, dozens of officers were walking around with pistols in their holsters, a fantastic status symbol.

Since these firearms were going mostly unused, I would approach officers before a driving mission and ask, "Hey, can I have your pistol for the day if you're not using it?" This was against protocol, of course, but I'd earned the trust of many officers. "Sure, Mitic. Here you go."

One day, I had a couple of majors riding in my back seat. Before setting out, I gave them my usual spiel about safety. "Gentlemen, as you know, we have not been issued the appropriate firearms to deal with a close-range conflict. During this trip, I'm asking you to take your pistols out of their holsters and keep them under your legs in case we run into trouble."

One of the majors said very firmly, "I will not do that, Corporal. That's an escalation in the rules of engagement."

"How is that an escalation in the rules of engagement? If there's no attack, there's no escalation," I replied.

"It is absolutely an escalation. And I'm going to report you for this," he said.

I looked at the major sitting next to him. "Sir, do you feel the same way?"

"Absolutely not, Corporal Mitic. My pistol is already out." That was the answer I was looking for, and if I hadn't gotten it, I wouldn't have taken them out on the mission.

"Thank you, Major," I said. "I'll get you safely to wherever you need to go." Then, to the first major, I said, "Lucky for you, your fellow passenger cares about our safety, so we'll take you out, too."

The major wasn't thrilled, but he never did report me.

In large group meetings, the other drivers and I routinely brought up the issue of inadequate weapons. During one such meeting, I remember the chief warrant officer telling us, "The thing you gotta remember about the C8s is that they might look sexy, but they don't have the range of a C7."

I responded by saying, "But if we get into a gunfight, it's going to be with some rebel across the street. We need close-range weapons we can pull out fast. We can't be fumbling around in the back seat looking for our weapons. It's got nothing to do with 'sexy.'"

But it didn't matter. We just kept hitting a brick wall on this issue. For years, a motto often repeated in the Canadian Armed Forces was "Improvise. Adapt. Overcome." This was a fancy way of saying we should make do with whatever tools we were given. But there was no way to improvise, adapt and overcome this particular problem, especially when an easy solution was sitting right in front of everyone. I felt if we didn't turn the heat up, we might be sorry too late.

One night, after our platoon warrant went to bed, I sat down in front of the computer in our tent and I wrote him a lengthy email detailing my concerns. I issued him an ultimatum, telling him that he either needed to stand up for us and tell the chain of command that we needed these weapons, or else maybe we weren't going to be so willing to drive around the streets of Kabul.

The warrant pulled me aside after receiving the email. "If this is going to be your attitude," he said, "maybe we should just send you home."

My jaw nearly hit the floor. "Really? You're going to send me home because I don't agree with you? What's your report going to say?" I asked. "That Jody has to go home because of an email?"

To his credit, the platoon warrant did work out a deal. We were issued two C8 rifles per section, to be carried by the co-driver sitting in the front passenger seat. And we finally got pistols as well—

brand-new Brownings, so fresh they were still in their packing grease. I'll admit that I carried myself with a bit of a swagger after that minor victory. And our drives felt a whole lot safer.

The fact that our drives were safer, though, didn't mean *we* always were. We got a small reminder of this one night in Camp Warehouse. My buddy Len and I were playing a video game inside our tent (I was playing a sniper, of course) when we heard a noise that sounded like fireworks—a loud hiss and then a pop followed by a whistle that got louder. We looked at each other.

"Is that incoming?" I asked.

"Sounds like," Len answered.

Sure enough, about twenty-five metres away from our tent, an enemy rocket landed. Fortunately, all our living areas were protected by defensive barriers called Hesco bastions. Steel mesh squares with burlap liners filled with dirt and gravel, these bastions absorbed a lot of the shrapnel and collateral material from the explosion. As soon as the rocket landed, panic spread through the camp. For a lot of us, this was the first time we had experienced an attack. But we had done drills for this, and so we followed our instructions.

The plan was for us to go up to the main Hesco bastion wall, crouch and lean against it. As I approached the wall, I was greeted by the odd sight of a whole bunch of soldiers awkwardly leaning against the wall as though they were sitting on invisible toilets. I looked at this line of guys and thought, "I'm not doing this." I headed back to my tent, put on my frag vest, grabbed my rifle, loaded it and headed to the main gate to repel any possible attack. There were a few other guys who were thinking the same thing, but the commanding officer and the sergeant major of the unit were already there. They demanded we return to our spots by the Hesco bastion wall, so we did.

As we were lined up against the wall, a couple of contract civilian workers heard a noise. It sure sounded like a car with bad suspension, but to them it was a rocket about to land on their heads. They panicked and dove on top of me, knocking me to the ground. I was buried at the bottom of a dog pile of these little civilian workers who were scared out of their trees. If another rocket had hit then, we would have all been blown to smithereens.

Fortunately, that was the last incoming rocket we dealt with at our camp, and the only person injured was a civilian contractor who got some debris lodged in his back. That was definitely one of our most exciting moments in Afghanistan.

•

My first tour in Afghanistan ended a few weeks later, and I headed back home to Petawawa. I was happy to see my girlfriend for the first time since our New Zealand getaway, but that happiness didn't last. I wish somebody had given me this advice before arriving home: a soldier needs about three months, give or take, to clear his head when he returns from active duty. For those first three months back, a soldier is not going to be him or herself.

I was still haunted by all the things I had witnessed in Kabul. Images played over and over in my head, whether it was small children begging for money, a mother holding a dead baby in the streets or my buddy T.J. bloodied up from a roadside bombing. My girlfriend expected me to return as the same guy who had left six months earlier, but I was a different man now, a different Jody.

Everything around me looked different, too. Maybe things hadn't changed much, but I felt like I was on an alien planet. My girlfriend had redecorated the house, moving some of the furniture around and repainting the bedroom, and I found it upset me. Life had gone on without me, and that fact was hard to take. People around me kept saying, "What's wrong with you, Jody? You've changed," and that would make me even more upset, not because they were wrong but because

I thought I was the kind of soldier who could just walk it off. But few soldiers can. It takes time after a tour of duty for a soldier to readjust to civilian life, and I wish I'd known that earlier. I was expected to continue life just as I had lived it before my tour, but I couldn't, not right away. I couldn't simply step back into a normal routine, as if I hadn't witnessed anything on mission. I couldn't just hop in the car and go grocery shopping like everything was fine.

That's what my girlfriend wanted and needed, and I can't blame her for that. She just wanted to pick up where we'd left off and carry on with our lives. She was starting to plan for our wedding, and shortly after I got back, she told me that the engagement ring she wanted was on sale for half price as a Valentine's Day promotion. I wasn't in the frame of mind to talk wedding stuff at that point and l told her I wasn't interested in buying the ring just then. Actually, I did want to buy one, but I wanted to choose it and at least surprise her a little bit.

A couple of weeks later, I went shopping and did buy the ring she wanted, but I didn't tell her. I put it in my sock drawer and debated about how and when I would give it to her. One night, we had friends over to our place for dinner. While she was complaining about how I wouldn't buy her the damn silly ring she wanted, I slipped away from the table and went to the bedroom. I came back out with the ring, got down on one knee in front of my girlfriend (and our guests) and asked, "So, will you marry me?" We all laughed as she accepted my "surprise" proposal.

My new fiancée was over-the-moon excited, but the feeling wouldn't last too long. As much as soldiers like to think they are hard-core superheroes, invincibility often disappears when we return home from a tour of duty. For me, planning for a wedding was just too much pressure at a moment when what I needed was time to re-cover. I often think of something Chief of the Defence Staff General Rick Hillier told us when he visited our base during my second tour to Afghanistan. He talked about calling home and talking to his wife, who told him the fridge was broken.

"No problem," he said to her. "We'll get a new one once I'm back."

"Actually, I went ahead and bought one already," his wife replied.

"Okay, great. I can use the old one as a beer fridge."

"Actually, I got rid of the old one already," his wife said.

Hillier used the exchange to demonstrate how soldiers want to play a part in what's going on at home even when they're far away. "But whoever's at home gets to make the home decisions," he said, stressing that there was no point telling family or anyone else back home how to conduct their daily lives if you weren't there. It was a great lesson he passed along that day—just one I could have used a bit earlier.

Another stressor on the home front was the fact that I was doing training for my infantry junior leadership course, and this was taking up a lot of my time. After I graduated, I was promoted to master corporal and was able to take a leadership position, which for me was an important step. But for my girlfriend it meant less time with me at a moment when she needed more. Things were getting increasingly tense between us, and they boiled over one night when she and I were out for dinner. She started crying and saying, "Who the fuck are you? Where is my Jody?"

Later, when we got home, I said, "I think it's in our best interest that we postpone the wedding. I just don't think we're in the right spot to get married right now."

She announced then that she was leaving. I was shocked, because I didn't want to break things off; I just wanted to postpone the wedding. But for her, this was all just too much. Our relationship was over.

While I wasn't certain this was the right time to get married, I *was* certain about one thing. I wanted to go back to Afghanistan—and this time as a sniper.

11

OPERATION ROCKET MAN

WHEN A soldier returns from an active mission like the one in Afghanistan, the army tries to give him or her a year or so at home before sending that soldier back to the battlefield. But these were busy times for the Canadian army, and in 2005, many soldiers were going back to Afghanistan after only a few months at home. Also, our tours of duty to Bosnia were continuing, which added to the workload of the Forces as a whole. This was all fine with me. I was eager to go back.

1 RCR was deployed, which gave me time to broaden my horizons as a sniper while I waited for my chance to leave. I took the new Sniper Detachment Commander's Course out at the Combat Training Centre in Gagetown, New Brunswick, which refreshed my basic training and also taught me how to be a team leader. A month later, I was back in Petawawa, and the place was a ghost town without 1 RCR there.

I was desperate to get back to Afghanistan, because our new chief of defence staff, General Rick Hillier, was saying and doing all the right things. He was constantly lobbying the Canadian government for more funds and resources for the Armed Forces. Finally, I thought we had a credible and authoritative military voice at the top of the chain of command. At Hillier's urging, a number of new airplanes and helicopters were ordered for the mission in Afghanistan. This gave us strategic lift capability—meaning that we had control over our supplies for the first time since the Korean War. With Hillier in charge, we were able to do things the right way.

We were constantly pushing to get more sniper spots on the tours because we were always short-handed. In an ideal world, we would have had about twenty snipers going over out of a group of 2500 total soldiers deployed. Better to be overstaffed and have extra soldiers ready to fill in when snipers went on leave, rather than be caught shorthanded. But after we completed extra training down in the States, we were told the next tour to Afghanistan would include a sniper team of only nine for a battle group of 2500—two teams of four, with a master sniper in charge.

It was determined that my pal Gord would be the overall sniper leader for the next tour to Afghanistan, which would deploy that summer. I was tabbed to be the leader of one of the two teams of four. But first, Gord and I were sent on our master sniper course at the army's Advanced Sniper School at CFB Gagetown. Not every sniper gets to become a master sniper. Timing and circumstance are big factors that play into who gets to go on the course. I got the thumbs-up, and was very pleased. But passing didn't mean I suddenly became part of some secret society with a secret handshake or hall of fame; it just meant I was qualified to do the paperwork associated with being in charge of a sniper section.

Next, our whole team of nine headed to CFB Wainwright, Alberta, to do some final preparations for our mission. We practised reconnaissance scenarios on fake villages prior to attack. My team had a couple of days to do reconnaissance of the village, which was being patrolled by some soldiers pretending to be the enemy force. We loved to mess with the guys playing the enemy. We'd steal their tooth-brushes or tie their bootlaces together—just fun, unexpected things to mess with their minds. Two days for a reconnaissance like this was way too long. We could have done it in just one night and then moved on to the next training exercise. Tired of waiting, I said to my team, "I'm going to walk down to the village right now."

One of my snipers said, "What do you mean? We're supposed to recce this place from afar."

"Well, that's no fun. Why don't we just walk down there and find out what's in that building?"

We knew the guys playing the enemy force didn't have night-vision goggles, so we walked down to the village, went into a couple of build-ings and did all of our reconnaissance work under the cloak of dark-ness. The next morning, I put together a detailed report of everything we saw. I explained to our commanders, "They've got some mortars, and here is where they have their bunks. And over behind this wall, they have a rocket launcher."

"How do you know all this?"

"Because we took a look last night," I said.

The commanders were not impressed. "Listen, Jody. Nobody would ever just walk into a Taliban village so easily, so don't be pulling those stunts during training. Play by the rules."

That was probably good advice, but I am not and never have been one to follow all rules just because they're rules. I operate according to the principle "If it's not specifically forbidden, it's authorized." Still, I knew my commander had a point. The situation over in Afghani-stan was heating up, and discipline would be required. In January, Glyn Berry, a Canadian diplomat, had been killed during a car-bomb attack that also severely wounded several soldiers. We were glued to the news coverage of the PPCLI soldiers in heavy combat against the Taliban. Later, just before our deployment at the end of the summer, we were very upset to hear that four members of the PPCLI unit were killed after they were ambushed by the Taliban inside a schoolhouse. Kandahar province was the Taliban heartland, and these guys were going to make us bleed for every inch; I was realizing that we were going to be engaged in intense combat this time around. And I couldn't wait.

In August we departed for Camp Mirage in Dubai. Camp Mirage was an open-secret military base—called Mirage even though most people knew of its existence. We used it as a final staging area before we were sent into Afghanistan. After a couple of days, we flew from there to Kandahar, where I began my first active mission as a sniper.

As soon as we landed, we connected with the PPCLI sniper team and started the transition process from their unit to ours so that they could go home for a much-needed rest after a six-month tour. The whole hand-over process had to be done very fast. One day the PPCLI snipers were in charge, and a couple of days later, it was 1 RCR's show to run. We did a couple of joint patrols, but there wasn't much time for anything else. They told us everything they'd learned, sharing their surveillance, reconnaissance and other intelligence. We had only a little crossover time between the two units, so we listened intently to everything the PPCLI had to say.

"Be forewarned," they said. "The Taliban are everywhere. And when you have an encounter with them—and you will—expect to see a large number of fighters." The Taliban's end game was to push us out of the area, so we were told to prepare to face a hundred fighters at a time.

After that, we spent a couple of days exploring Kandahar Airfield. It was really nice. The buildings were air-conditioned. We had Internet. The barracks were like condos. Since we were snipers, we had special privileges. We slept two men to a room instead of the usual four. That meant we got a bunk bed each, so we laid all our equipment up on the top bunk and slept on the bottom one. I slept in that room a total of about fifteen times during my entire mission of about five months, but my extra equipment, which I stored there, was very comfortable for the duration of its stay.

Kandahar Airfield had some other Canadian comforts, too—including a Tim Hortons outlet. The lines for Tim's were always long because American, British and Australian soldiers had developed a taste for our coffee and doughnuts. It was way better than drinking bad coffee out of a Ziploc boil bag, which is what we had to do while on mission. One time, Barry and I were in line when a pudgy American air force soldier ahead of us ordered a Boston cream doughnut.

"Sorry, we're all out."

Upon receiving this news, this guy lost the power of speech. His spirit was completely crushed. His shoulders slumped, and as he leaned on the counter, he started to tremble. He acted the way a spoiled child reacts to not getting a toy, but this was a grown-ass man in a uniform, with a gun under his shoulder. Barry and I couldn't help but laugh.

•

One of our first assignments in Kandahar was "Operation Rocket Man." We were constantly facing rocket attacks on our base at the Kandahar Airfield, much like the one I'd experienced towards the end of my tour in Kabul, but these attacks were more frequent. Every couple of days a rocket would fly over the base. Sometimes, they would land and cause some damage, but oftentimes they missed their mark completely. It was almost like the enemy was using the Wile E. Coyote method of launching rockets, by setting them up against a rock, lighting the fuse, running away and hoping for the best. Whoever our

Rocket Man was, accuracy was definitely not his strong suit. He did, however, succeed at causing chaos. Having rocket alarms going off at our base at all hours was probably an intentional psychological warfare tactic. When we'd hear the alarm, we'd have to run to a bunker.

The problem was that by the time the alarm went off, we often didn't have enough time to get to a bunker. The truth for soldiers on base was this: by the time the first rocket landed, we were already at the mercy of luck and fate. Also, combat arms soldiers tended to have a laissez-faire attitude towards the rocket attacks, whereas those who never left the wire around the Forward Operating Base—or FOBits, as we called them—would run to the bunkers immediately in full protective gear. If Gord and I were chilling and having a coffee when the alarms went off, we didn't always rush to the bunker. It's not that we weren't taking the attacks seriously; it's just that we became a bit immune to them, and running to the bunker meant we'd be stuck there for about forty-five minutes while we waited to be given the all-clear. Sometimes, taking our chances and chilling with a cup of coffee just seemed like a better plan.

Another better plan was trying to stop the rockets from landing in the first place, which is what we attempted. Together with the Royal Air Force snipers who were responsible for security around the airfield, we went on a mission to hunt down Wile E. Rocket Man by saturating the area with a sniper presence. We decided to break out into three three-man teams instead of two four-man teams and a stay-back commander. This was our first mission outside of Kandahar Airfield as snipers, the pop-our-cherry mission for our Canadian group. Working with the British forces was pretty cool, because they had a lot of experience and we got to use a bunch of equipment that we had only trained with a little bit previously—such as suppressors, or silencers, for our rifles, improved radios and night-vision goggles.

The difference between training and being in the theatre of war is that in training we had maybe one piece of night-vision to every four soldiers, but on the mission, suddenly we had one each. Because we weren't used to employing night-vision all the time in training, we left camp that night with the devices in our pockets, while all the British snipers set out with theirs strapped on. As we were getting ready to head outside the wire, the British head sniper stopped me and asked, "Excuse me, don't you have any night-vision with you?"

"Yes sir," I said, and tapped the pocket on the front of my chest. "I have 'em right here."

"You're not going to wear them?"

"I'll just pull them out when I need them."

I'm fairly sure this guy thought we were morons. He was probably happy that he was heading out in a different direction and that we were on our own. Beyond the wire, it was a pitch-black, clear, moonless night. I couldn't even see my hand in front of my own face. Barry, Kash and I stumbled around in the dark trying to get to our position. We had used aerial surveillance to study the area before heading out, but something had changed since the last check—a whole bunch of tents had appeared out of nowhere. Barry turned to me. "Holy shit," he whispered. "I think we just stumbled into a Bedouin camp." It turned out that a Bedouin tribe had very recently settled into a spot just outside of the Kandahar Airfield.

We decided to move away from their camp, as we were quite certain our Rocket Man wasn't a nomadic tribesman. Soon after, we heard barking and realized that the Bedouin dogs, kept for the purpose of scaring away intruders, were hot on our trail. We picked up the pace, as much as one can when travelling in the pitch dark, but the barking was getting louder and louder, and then turned into mean and nasty growling, as if these beasts were on the hunt of their lives.

"Barry, Kash," I said. "You guys keep going. I'll deal with these dogs." It's a wonder the guys could hear me over the snarling and growling and breathing that emerged from the darkness behind us. These dogs were in a very vicious mood, so vicious that I suddenly realized we could be torn limb from limb if I didn't act fast. For a moment, I had a flashback to Kosovo. I thought to myself, "Ah fuck. I don't want to have to shoot at another dog."

I raised my C8 carbine rifle—which had the suppressor on it— and flicked the safety to semi-automatic. The snarling was really close now. You know a dog is pissed off and out for blood when he snarls while breathing in instead of while breathing out. Using "the force," I tried to sense where the dogs were in the dark. When I thought I had their approach picked out, I fired off about two rounds a dozen metres in front of me. They weren't that loud, because of the suppressor, so it sounded more like a nail gun. As the bullets hit the ground, the light dust, which was like talcum powder, rose in a cloud that was visible against the dark sky. Just then, I saw the silhouette of a black dog run past the dust cloud. That dog was humongous. It was so big it looked like a fucking horse. It didn't like the fact that I was shooting right at it, and it turned away from me, giving me one last snarl before running off. I was pretty relieved to hear those beasts retreating.

I headed back to Barry and Kash, who were a hundred metres or so away. They were prone with their rifles cocked. They had their night-vision on now, too, so they could see me coming.

"What happened?" they asked.

"Didn't you guys hear me shoot?"

"No," they said. I now had to get on the radio and call our units to the left and right to explain why they'd heard shots. This was going to be embarrassing, because if they'd heard the shots, that meant the Taliban could have, too, and if that were the case, our mission was probably compromised.

"Hey, did you guys just hear anything?" I said over the radio. I was expecting to hear, "What the fuck are you guys shooting at over there?" but instead, the answer I got was, "Didn't hear anything, mate. What's up?"

"Uh . . . nothing," I said. "All good. Just checking in." That's when it dawned on us just how effective suppressors are.

We spent the rest of that night out there, hoping that one of the teams might catch Wile E. Coyote, but we never did get him. Even if we had caught him, the truth was that another guy would have set up after him and done the same thing. Though we never caught our Rocket Man, we did learn a whole lot of lessons on that first mission. Needless to say, we never again left camp at night without night-vision . . . and a few dog treats.

•

A couple of days later, we received word from the commanding officer—rather abruptly—that we needed to be out at Patrol Base Wilson, an Afghan police station about an hour's drive from Kandahar that was a stronghold for Canadian Forces. The base was named after Canadian Master Corporal Timothy Wilson, who had died earlier that year after being injured in a vehicle crash. Patrol Base Wilson was being mortared on a daily basis by the Taliban. The attacks were almost like clockwork—one around ten in the morning, and another one around four in the afternoon. Our job as snipers was to help pinpoint where these guys were launching from. The base didn't have a lot of defence mechanisms like sandbags or Hesco bastions, so it was vulnerable. We shipped out immediately, not knowing how long we'd be gone.

That quickly put an end to the relatively luxurious sleeping quarters we'd had at the Kandahar base. At Patrol Base Wilson, we slept in a big tent covered in blast blankets in case one of the mortars landed nearby. If we came under attack, we were to run out of the tents and get into the armoured G Wagons just outside, which could withstand a decent-sized blast.

As for our assignment, we were to keep watch from the tower for Taliban spotters who were helping with the placement of the mortars. We were given orders to shoot anyone who appeared to be a spotter. There was just one problem with that: the area beyond Patrol Base Wilson consisted of a number of villages, and there was a good chance innocent people—maybe even children—might poke their heads above walls once they heard a mortar explosion. Standard operating procedure was to shoot at anyone we saw, but in actuality, we made split-second decisions based on who we saw pop up.

The Taliban enjoyed testing our security, just to see how close they could get to us. They would sometimes strap wires and what looked like a wearable bomb onto a mentally challenged person from the area. Then they'd coax this civilian to walk towards the checkpoint and not stop under any circumstances. The troops would yell at the person, telling him to stop, but often, he'd just keep walking, having not the faintest idea that he was being used as a pawn. Unfortunately, these innocents would often be gunned down because we didn't know if their explosives were real or fake. Meanwhile, the Taliban would be hiding near enough to carefully note how close the civilian got before he was shot. If he made it to about fifty metres from the security zone, they knew they had to make a bomb that had a blast radius of about a hundred metres if they wanted to do significant damage next time. Because of recurring incidents like these, we had to be very strict at checkpoints. We were constantly worried about the threat of suicide bombers, both on foot and in vehicles. We didn't take any chances, and even stopped vehicles we knew to be local police cars, just to be safe.

Just before we'd arrived, the captain of the local police tried to drive through our checkpoint without stopping. He probably figured that because he was with the police and in a marked car, he could just run through with no issues. When he failed to heed warnings from the guards and didn't stop his car, the guards opened fire and killed him. It turns out this captain was a relative of the local chief of police. The police chief showed up at Patrol Base Wilson a few days later with a group of his officers who looked ready to get into a gunfight. We went up to the rooftop of the patrol base and got into our sniper positions just in case. The Afghan National Police were our allies, and Patrol Base Wilson was shared between us, but at that moment, they were so upset by the loss of one of their men that we just didn't know what would happen. As it turned out, they were there mostly to express their anger, which was understandable, given they'd just lost a fellow officer. Our chain of command was able to talk with the local police chief and explain our soldiers' actions, which helped lessen the tension.

We avoided the gunfight in that scenario, but the daily mortar attacks on the base continued, and we hadn't been able to locate where they were coming from. One day, an attack happened about half an hour outside the usual schedule. I was in the tent sleeping when the mortars started falling all around our base. I grabbed my helmet and my frag vest and headed out to our armoured vehicle. I was inside, safe and sound, when Dave Sloaner, one of our snipers, rapped on the window.

"Any room in there for Sloaner?" he said, putting on his best puppy-dog eyes. We had room for him, but it meant moving equipment out of the back seat into the trunk. I jumped out and opened the back and we both began tossing radios and other gear into the trunk as fast as we could. At that exact moment, a mortar hit just a few metres away. It was so close that we felt the heat from the explosion and the concussion blast. Ready or not, Dave and I jumped into the G Wagon. We waited out the mortars, and despite the near miss, we were giggling like schoolgirls. After a few minutes, we noticed our vehicle slowly start to sink to the left.

Once the mortar attack had ended and it was deemed safe to leave the vehicle, we jumped out to see why we were leaning. Sure enough, the back left tire had been hit by shrapnel and was completely shredded. Dave and I looked at each other. "Holy shit, man," I said. That tire was situated exactly in between where Dave and I had been standing as we tossed gear into the trunk. Miraculously, the shrapnel had missed our legs and destroyed the tire. Dave found the impact site of the mortar five metres from where we had been standing.

"Close call," he said. That was an understatement. We didn't say much else about the incident, but we both knew we'd been lucky.

The next day there was a patrol through what we called Ambush Alley. Filled with trees and marijuana plants, Ambush Alley was an ideal location in which Taliban fighters could hide. The mission that day was to locate some Taliban fighters and fire at them in an attempt to push them out of the area. Naturally, as a sniper, I wanted to be included in this mission, but I had to make a case for why. That's the funny thing about being a sniper. You're often invited on as support, but you're an add-on to the team, an outsider. Officers want you there to assist, but sometimes they're not sure how to best use your skill set. This time, I was able to talk my way into one of the armoured vehicles and secure spots in another one for Barry and Kash. I was pretty excited about this because it looked like it could be our first opportunity to have a real encounter with the enemy force close up.

I was seated in the back of a LAV—a light armoured vehicle—run by a platoon commander everybody called Captain America. This guy had a shaved head, had played college football and was always trying to be super-hard-core and keen. Captain America turned to me, the rookie in his LAV, and said, "Whatever happens, we're going to let the twenty-five millimetre cannon handle the situation. Clear?"

"Okay, no problem," I responded. I put on my earplugs, because if this cannon was fired, it was going to be extremely loud.

We pulled out of the camp, made a right turn and travelled maybe five hundred metres before our LAV slowed down because there were Taliban fighters on the side of the road. One of them was dressed head to toe in white linen and he was standing out in the field by himself, with a great big grin on his face. It was one of the weirdest, most eerie things I've ever seen. Our LAV vehicles pulled up beside him, but he wasn't moving, and he still had the weird smile glued to his face. Then all of his buddies started yelling at him from behind this mud and rock area about fifty metres away. Clearly, they were telling him to hurry his ass over to where they were. It was like he was late for the ambush, but he didn't seem to care.

I had my rifle on me and I thought to myself, "I've got an open shot and it's clear he's the enemy. I'm just going to shoot this prick now."

But as I started to pull my rifle up, Captain America grabbed my arm. "Put it down," he said. "Remember what I said about the cannon?" I shrugged and crouched down.

As the turret rotated and aimed the cannon, the Taliban started shooting at our vehicles. This was the first time I faced enemy gunfire in the heat of battle.

"The cannon is jammed!" the gunner yelled from the turret.

I stood up and was about to aim my rifle again when Captain America stopped me a second time. "Just let the cannon do its thing."

"The cannon's not doing jack shit right now," I said.

Fortunately for us, the LAVs in front of us and behind us had functional cannons and started firing away. The Taliban fighters were shooting with Russian machine guns that didn't stand a chance against heavy cannon fire. They quickly retreated.

When we returned to our base, we lined up all the LAVs in a row in the parking area. I walked the length of the convoy—maybe eight to ten LAVs in total—and didn't find a single scratch or bullet hole on any of our vehicles. I had a tremendous amount of respect for the

Taliban as soldiers, but their shooting skills left a lot to be desired. It seemed that instead of actually aiming, they preferred to pull the trigger and spray bullets into the air, hoping the bullets might hit a target.

The bullets missed us on that occasion, but we were about to be introduced to a different type of warfare, one that would put us directly in the line of much more dangerous enemy fire.

12

OPERATION MEDUSA

IN AUGUST of 2006, the PPCLI Recce platoon had secured a local educational facility known as "the white schoolhouse," located in the Panjwaii district of Afghanistan. Taliban fighters counterattacked by launching a volley of RPGs—rocket-propelled grenades—into the school, killing four Canadian soldiers and wounding many others from the PPCLI. The PPCLI fought ferociously, but recce platoons travel light to move fast and they hadn't planned for an extended battle. Also, a shortage of ammo and water forced them to reluctantly retreat, for the time being.

After the heavy fighting, the insurgents regained control of the schoolhouse, and NATO was forced to come up with a new strategy for getting the Taliban out of the Panjwaii district. That is when Operation Medusa was hatched—so named because tactically we needed to stop slaying individual snakes and this time slice off the entire head of the beast. This Canadian-led NATO operation was going to be different from anything we'd done so far. It was a bit of a wake-up call. So was the fact that my buddy Jeff Walsh had been killed in friendly fire in an accident that happened in August. Clearly we were entering a high-risk situation. That didn't deter me in any way; if anything, it made my resolve stronger. I'd trained for this and I was ready.

The Taliban fighters in the Panjwaii area appeared to be numerous, determined and well organized. The offensive against them marked the first time Canadian soldiers had been involved in a ground assault of this magnitude since the Korean War. When we were getting our marching orders back at Kandahar Airfield, it became clear that each rifle company—Alpha, Bravo and Charles—wanted its own sniper unit for the mission. I led the sniper team with Barry and Kash for Charles Company. Our offensive and our first goal—known as Objective Rugby—was to take back the white schoolhouse. As you can imagine, there was considerable excitement among us to be involved in such a significant offensive. For me personally, this was why I had spent more than a decade training in the Armed Forces—to have this kind of ground opportunity. That schoolhouse had become a symbolic building for all of us, representing not only the Taliban's resistance but the loss of four of our soldiers. Reclaiming it meant getting something back for them, a tribute to what they had accomplished that we were left to uphold in their names.

So when our commanding officer, Major Matthew Sprague, explained the mission, I expected a call to honour, an *Any Given Sunday* type of pep talk. But Major Sprague's speech was very measured and deliberate. Don't get me wrong: I have a ton of respect for Major Sprague, but I was surprised that his pre-offensive speech was so muted. On top of that, he gave an order that left a lot of us scratching our heads. "If anybody gets hurt during this mission," he said, "we're going to stop right away and take care of it. We are going to make sure the casualties are dealt with and then reassess the situation before moving forward."

Wasn't the whole point of a ground assault to create heavy momentum and push forward? In some ways, it almost sounded like a contradiction: "Let's not take any casualties, but let's try to kill the enemy."

After the speech, Barry came over to me and said, "Either we're going to kick some ass—or we're going to get our asses kicked. It's one or the other."

Kash leaned in. "I think there are going to be a lot of people killed in this attack."

Our job as snipers was to look at the battle plan for Charles Company and see how we could help them reach their objectives. The best way for us to help was to get to an elevated position around our soldiers. That way, we could keep watch and warn them about what was coming up ahead. From that vantage point, we would also be able to shoot at the enemy and provide cover for our troops, if either was needed. A group of Joint Task Force snipers was about to get on a plane to go home, but when orders for Operation Medusa came in, they stayed behind and joined us.

Before the mission started, we performed a "leaders' recce." The commanding officer, all the company commanders, the artillery commander, the engineering commander and the sniper-team leaders went out in vehicles to scout out the potential battlefield at Masum Ghar. There were quite a few of us, and we didn't want to draw the attention of the enemy, so we tried to be as discreet as possible. I'm surprised the Taliban didn't shoot at us while we were doing this recce mission, but for some reason they never did.

Masum Ghar is a fairly big mountain. I decided it would be the best spot for us to set up home base. The JTF2 sniper leader agreed. My group would set up about halfway up the mountain close to Charles company, while the JTF team would go even higher since their communications equipment was able to work at a higher altitude than ours. Having the JTF guys above us meant they had our backs, so that was cool with us.

After all of our spots were picked out, we headed back to Kandahar Airfield for final preparations. We were told to pack about a week's worth of supplies—clothes, toiletries and anything else we would require. The plan was to be in the Masum Ghar area for about three days of preparation, with the ground assault happening on the fourth day. In an ideal world, the entire Objective Rugby—taking back the schoolhouse and re-establishing control of the area—would take about seven days. As experienced as I was in packing for sniper missions, I was green when it came to packing for an operation like this. I wanted to make sure I was well stocked. I packed extra batteries for my radio, four gallons of water and as much ammo as I could fit in every single pocket.

We departed Kandahar just before Labour Day, heading out at night for a "leaguer," which is when troops form a provisional camp by parking together in one spot overnight. As we hung around the vehicles, the engineers did a sweep of the area with mine detectors.

I asked one of the engineers, "Hey bro, do you really think there are mines around here?"

"Yeah, we think so," he responded, looking at me sideways from underneath his helmet as though I was an idiot. At that very second, his sweeper started beeping. "There's one right here," he said nonchalantly. He pulled out a can of orange spray paint and marked the spot where the land mine was buried. I felt a bit foolish for asking my question, but I didn't say anything. All I could think was, "Holy shit, the entire company is parked on a minefield." Whether it was bravado or complete ignorance, nobody else seemed overly concerned. We were simply told to avoid stepping anywhere near the spray-painted areas the engineers had identified.

As we were getting ready the next morning to push ahead to Masum Ghar, dozens upon dozens of vehicles passed us—filled with hundreds of fighting-age males who were probably Taliban fighters, though they were unarmed. They stared at us as they drove past, but what we noticed was that they were heading the wrong way. It's like they were getting the hell out of Dodge before all hell broke loose. We had put out strong signals that we were coming in for an aggressive assault, so maybe the word that we meant business was spreading. Maybe they were trying to minimize their losses. Instead of having a thousand soldiers die, it was in their best interests to have only a hundred killed.

As they fled in the opposite direction, we headed to our battle position at Masum Ghar. We pulled into our spot and the ramp for our vehicle dropped. It was time to head out to our designated positions. For me and my sniper unit, that meant we had to trek up the side of the mountain. I sat on the ramp and looped my arms through the shoulder straps of my rucksack, then I went to stand up—and couldn't. I had packed so much into that rucksack that it probably weighed over a hundred pounds. One of the boys came down the ramp laughing. "Let me help ya out there, Jody!" He grabbed me and hoisted me to my feet.

"Thanks, bro," I grunted. We both chuckled and gave each other knuckles. "Stay safe, brother," he said. I winked at him, turned and headed up the mountain.

As I stared up the side of the mountain, I realized I had a pretty big dilemma on my hands. If I could barely stand wearing this heavy rucksack, how on earth was I going to walk uphill with it? Clearly, I'd made the rookie mistake of packing too much stuff for my first field assault. Maybe the adrenaline helped, because somehow I was able to head up the slope with Barry and Kash. But as we approached our preselected site, I noticed that it was already occupied. A bunch of Afghan National Army, or ANA, soldiers were in our spot, alongside a couple of American soldiers. The ANA soldiers were always accompanied by one or two senior American officers who oversaw what they were doing. In this case, Dexter, an old, grizzled American captain, was in charge. I had met Dexter a few days earlier during the recce.

"Hey Dexter," I said, "I think your ANA guys are in our spot."

"Okay, we'll move out," he responded, and soon enough, they did. Once they were gone, I saw why this spot was so amazing. Not only did it have a bird's-eye view of the river valley and the battleground below, it also had an overhang of rocks, which made for a nice shaded resting spot.

Once we were alone, we started doing what snipers do in these situations: planning. We mapped out the area from our vantage point and started doing up our range cards. This helped us get a better understanding of the terrain and more quickly identify the area where a target might be. We laser-measured targets for a more accurate idea of the distances we were dealing with. That way, if we saw an enemy fighter standing next to a rock or a tree, we could quickly calculate how far away he was from us. But the enemy was pretty far away. We figured the closest stronghold was at a distance of approximately 1800 metres, so shooting them from our position was going to be pretty tough. From what we could see, though, there was a lot of movement at the enemy base.

The other units were also getting into position. LAV IIIs and Coyote armoured reconnaissance and surveillance vehicles were moving to their spots, while the artillery guys were doing their final preparations as well. The artillery forward observation officer, or FOO, was starting to call in preparatory artillery strikes. It was a free-fire zone, so anyone who thought they had a target was allowed to take a shot. While everybody prepped the target area for the battle ahead, Kash noticed something in the distance: a bunch of enemy fighters in a farmer's field. When I'd been looking through the binos earlier, I hadn't seen anything, but that was typical. Barry and I could spend hours at the glass and see absolutely nothing, but the second Kash picked up a pair of binoculars, out came the enemy. On this day, Kash's eagle eyesight came in handy, and as usual, he spotted Taliban fighters before anybody else did.

When we watched them further, it became evident that these guys were keeping an eye on Canadian movement. They were looking through their own binoculars and using their radios to relay information. They were about three thousand metres away.

I radioed the artillery FOO at the bottom of the hill. I wanted to call in some heavy artillery, the new M777, from the Canadian 155 howitzer battery that had positioned itself next to Patrol Base Wilson for Operation Medusa. "I have a fire mission for you, what appears to be a reinforced enemy position," I said. I started the procedure to call in an artillery strike, giving the enemy's map grid, position, compass bearing and distance.

"I can't see them from here," the artillery commander interrupted me.

Of course he couldn't see them. He was sitting on a lawn chair next to his vehicle half as high up the mountain as I was. "That's fine. I have clear view. Clearly an enemy position. Fire mission. Over," I said into the radio.

There was a long pause, and I could see him looking through his binos in the direction of the enemy. "I still can't see them," he repeated.

"Yes, I understand." I kept my tone diplomatic but forceful. "But I have clear view. I'm the sniper team. We just need the green light."

"It's day one here," he said. "We don't have a lot of ammo and we want to try to conserve it."

I wasn't sure what that had to do with us calling in an artillery barrage on Taliban fighters. I was getting to the point where I wanted to run down to the bottom of the mountain and head-butt this guy.

A couple of minutes later, he came back over the radio. "Okay, here's what we can do. I can give you six rounds." That translated to twenty-four rounds, because it's six rounds times four guns in the battery. If we couldn't nail these guys with twenty-four rounds, then the gods of war were smiling on them, not us. But then he added, "That's six rounds total."

"Six rounds?" I said. "Including corrections?" You always need to take a round or two and then correct your shot based on the round's proximity to the target. If we had only six rounds total, that would leave probably four to fire for effect on the enemy.

"Yes, six rounds total. Including corrections," he barked back.

Fine. It was better than nothing. The first round I called in clearly got the enemy's attention. It landed within two hundred metres of them, and it's kind of hard not to notice when a 155 millimetre howitzer shell lands that close to you. Most of the guys started scurrying off, looking for cover or heading to their bunker areas. But there was this one fighter dressed in camouflage with a scarf around his neck and a round hat on his head. While everybody else was fleeing the area, he was just standing there as if nothing was happening. I had four rounds left and was on target, so I made the radio call for effect, thereby unleashing the artillery to fire their rounds as quickly as possible, completely saturating the area with explosions and shrapnel— well, in this case, four rounds' worth—aimed right where the guy with the scarf was standing.

As I heard artillery going off in the distance, the Taliban fighter turned and started to casually stroll away, unfazed when more rounds landed all around him. One of the blast forces blew his scarf off his shoulder. He readjusted it, flicking it over his shoulder in an almost "fuck you" manner, and continued his stroll as the four rounds finished landing. With no more artillery to call in, all I could do was watch him walk away. That's an image that will be burned into my brain for the rest of my life.

This is me on my BMX bike around age seven.

(*From left to right*) My dad, Hemi Mitic; my sister, Katie; me; my mom, Joanne Fisher; and my brother, Cory, in 1987. I was ten years old.

Me in front of a real-life fighter jet at CFB Borden, north of Toronto. My uncle Jim was in the Forces and took me on this memorable tour.

At battle school in Meaford. The boys and I are taking a break from the endless cleaning and re-cleaning of the "shacks," otherwise known as barracks.

This is my bunk layout, ready for inspection in the barracks in Meaford. Well . . . at least *I* thought it was ready for inspection, but whoever had a look might not have agreed.

Me during our final training exercise at Meaford. This exercise lasted about a week, and as you can see, it didn't involve much sleeping.

Me and the battle school boys in one of the trenches we not only dug but lived in for the duration of the exercise.

Here I am during a field training mission at Marine Corps Base Camp Lejeune in North Carolina, with my precious C7 in hand and my war face on.

One of my buddies (*right*) and me (*left*) with scrim on our helmets to keep us camouflaged. I've got a *B* for Bravo Company emblazoned on my hand.

Me (*left*) and the commanding officer at the battle school in Meaford. He's presenting me with a trophy for Top Shot. This is the same man who, a year earlier, kicked me off the base but later gave me a second chance.

My platoon mates and me in Kosovo. I'm second from the left.

Patrolling through a building
in Kosovo.

I'm standing on a Russian-made
self-propelled artillery piece
left behind when the Serbs
evacuated Kosovo. Anti-tank
rocket in hand, I'm having some
fun pretending I'm the brave
armour hunter who destroyed
this burnt-out tank.

At Patrol Base Wilson. This is the truck that was fired upon when a captain of the local police failed to stop at a checkpoint.

Here's a G Wagon at Patrol Base Wilson. This is the typical condition of vehicles we used there, because they were employed not only as means of transportation but as bunkers during mortar attacks.

Before Operation Rocket Man, right at the beginning of our tour in Afghanistan. These are my guys, the sniper team, standing in front of a Voodoo 5 American helicopter. (*From left to right*) Me, Gord, Kash, Barry, Dave, Steve, Senan and "B" (Yves).

This is a land mine, similar to the one that I stepped on. The gun is laid next to it for scale.

The best three-man sniper team ever—Barry (*left*), solid, tough, pragmatic, naturally fit, a real soldier's soldier; me (*middle*); and Kash (*right*), a smart, inquisitive, curious and laid-back Jamaican killing machine.

Our sniper team went out on a six-man patrol and stopped for a selfie in a typical Afghan barn.

Kash and I are on the side of Masum Ghar, on the lookout for bad guys. As you can see by the Pepsi, it was very tough going.

Taking a break on one of the first days of Operation Medusa.

Keeping watch during Operation Medusa. I was hunkered down for another long day, boots undone, radio in hand, rifle nearby.

That's me, aka "little brother," and "big brother" Rob, commander of the Green Berets, on a mission around Sperwan Ghar.

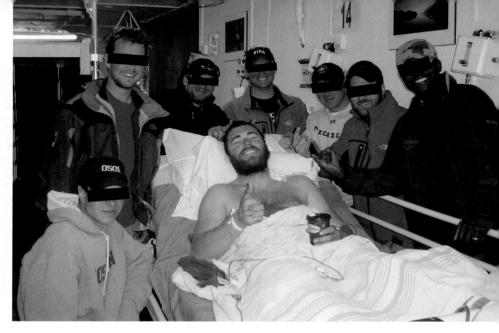

This photo was taken the day after I stepped on a land mine. I'm at
the base hospital at Kandahar, surrounded by my team, drinking my
last Kandahar coffee before heading to Canada.

Here I am, pumped full of blood thinners and pain meds, getting out of
the Challenger. I was about to see my friends and family for the first time
post-injury, and then be taken to Sunnybrook hospital in Toronto.

Me during the Achilles 5k run in support of St. John's Rehab in March 2009.

Errol McGihon/Sun Media

Jim Wilkes/Toronto Star

I was really moved to be invited to Scarborough Kennedy Public School while I was still recovering from my injuries. These kids made my day.

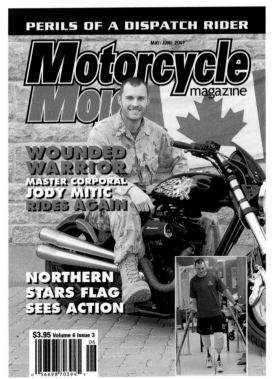

That's me riding the bike of my dreams, which the great guys at Harley-Davidson had custom-made for me—complete with a thumb-shift.

Cover photo: Glenn Roberts; Inset: Craig Robertson/Sun Media

Governor General Michaëlle Jean presented me with the Sacrifice Medal in November 2009. Looking on are Prime Minster Stephen Harper (*right*) and Chief of Defence Staff General Walter Natynczyk (*left*).

Standing, holding Aylah, beside a monument to one of my heroes, Terry Fox. He was someone I'd looked up to since I was a kid, but after I lost part of my legs, the significance of his run really hit home with me.

The best volunteers ever helped me get elected to the Innes Ward of Ottawa in 2014. I went from hiding away to standing out and standing up, for myself and for others. That's why I chose bright yellow as my campaign colour.

Me and my beautiful wife, Alannah.

Alannah and me in uniform with our two girls on Remembrance Day 2013 at the Canadian War Museum.

I turned to Barry and Kash. "Did you see that? That guy's got balls of steel! I love that fucking guy!" That was the last I saw of him.

Our first night on the side of the mountain was as adventure-filled as the day—but for different reasons. We slept in shifts at night, and each of us had a two-hour patrol and four hours of sleep. While I was on patrol that night, nature called. I had my little Ziploc bag with me, and inside were a couple of "toilet tickets" and some wet-wipes. I headed out to do my business. The moonlight was pretty intense that night, so I didn't wear my night-vision goggles or use a flashlight. After finding a good spot, I tossed my Ziploc onto the ground and started to take off my gear. It's not that easy being a soldier in this situation, because you have to drop your rifle, your frag vest and a whole bunch of other stuff before you can get down to business. Finally, I was all set and started to squat—but then I heard a distinct crunching noise very close by. Then I heard crackling. And it was getting louder. I froze. "What the fuck is that noise?" I thought to myself. "Someone crumpling paper? But why would somebody be doing that at two in the morning?"

The sound continued. I started to reach down for my rifle when I suddenly recognized the sound. It was thin plastic being shredded. I looked down and realized that my Ziploc bag of toiletries was covered in massive black ants. They were swarming the Ziploc, and their teeth were so big they were actually crunching through the plastic. The sheer number of these insects was mind-boggling. I'd chosen a terrible spot for what I needed to do: a thriving anthill.

I looked down at my boots, where a bunch of ferocious black ants were now crawling onto me. I jumped up and started stomping wildly to get them off. I still hadn't done what I came out there to do. But to do that, I needed my Ziploc bag, which was still covered in ants. I put on my combat gloves and pulled out my Gerber tool, which was equipped with a pair of pliers. I carefully picked up the Ziploc bag with the pliers and I smashed it against the ground over and over again. The mandibles of the ants were so strong that it took me a while to knock them all off. Finally, my boots and Ziploc were clean, and I decided I'd better find another location for my solo mission.

•

The unpleasant ant experience, coupled with minimal sleep, put me in a foul mood the next day. I actually got into a bit of an argument with Warrant Officer Rick Nolan, who was the quartermaster for Charles Company. I had known Rick for quite a while—I trained under him with the recce platoon—and knew him to be a stand-up guy. We needed to get some supplies delivered to us at the side of the mountain and he wanted us to come down from our position to get them.

"Can you at least drive them to the base of the mountain for us?" I asked.

"Why can't you just come down here and get them yourselves?" he fired back.

Maybe I wasn't the only one who had had a bad night. Or maybe tensions were running high because we all knew that the attack was imminent. I went down the mountain to get the supplies, and they were waiting right where I'd asked Rick to leave them. Still, it took me three trips to get all the supplies back up to our sniper position.

It was now our second day in position. It was still dark, but I noticed there was a ton of activity and a buzz at the base of the mountain. Vehicles were starting up and soldiers were bustling about, packing up their gear. Why were they gearing up when we were still about twenty-four hours away from our scheduled offensive attack?

I turned to Kash, who had been on watch the last few hours. "Did you hear anything over the radio that would prompt all that action?"

"Nope. Nothing at all," he responded.

I picked up my radio and called down to Major Sprague. "This is

6-3 Charlie. What's going on down there?" We always used our call signs when addressing each other over the radio.

"Pack up. Get down here. We're going in," Major Sprague replied.

"Has there been a change of plans?" I asked again.

"Don't have time to explain. Just get your asses down here now," he ordered.

"Roger that," I said.

We quickly packed up all of our gear. For whatever reason, the schedule had been moved up by about a day. We came down the mountain and we were going to join the platoon at the base, but just before we got to the bottom, I got this weird feeling. I knew the area was secure, but I decided to call in on the radio and alert everybody that we were approaching, just in case.

"All call signs 3, this is 6-3 Charlie. We are approaching you from your left flank position. Please acknowledge."

I got a couple of confirmations from the radio. We had the all-clear to approach. It was a good thing I got clearance on the radio because I was told later that a couple of our guys spotted us in their thermal binoculars and were preparing to take us out.

I found Major Sprague sitting inside the command hatch of his LAV, putting on his helmet. This was a man who was carrying the weight of leading the first deliberate Canadian assault since Korea.

"What's going on here?" I asked.

"Well, we're going in now," he responded. He was doing up his chin strap but you could tell his mind was ten steps ahead, thinking about all the things that could happen once we crossed the Arghandab River. As the saying goes, "No plan lasts longer than first contact with the enemy." And Major Sprague knew it.

"Any other changes to the plan besides the time?"

"No. All the same." He made an effort to focus on me for a second, his sniper-team leader. "So what do you want to do?" he asked.

"Let's stick to the original plan," I said. "You guys take Objective Rugby. Once the white schoolhouse is secure, my team and I will go to the roof, set up our sniper position and cover you as you move to the next objective."

"Good to go," Major Sprague said. "Fall in with the battle captain's LAV and let's roll."

Captain Trevor Norton would be in charge of the armoured vehicles once the troops dismounted. In ground-fighting situations, the LAVs become a mobile heavy weapons fire base. You manoeuvre them to an area and concentrate their fire to suppress the enemy in the target area. The troops on foot can then start advancing, with the fire base shifting fire to always be in front of them. This is a technique Canadians mastered in World War I.

Before getting into the LAV, I took a good look at the vehicles around us. I was surprised by the lack of combat engineering vehicles such as combat bulldozers and obstacle-clearing equipment. What we did have was what appeared to be a Zettelmeyer front-loader. It was painted green and had what we call "hillbilly armour"—steel welded into place to provide some kind of protection, added at the last minute. We also had a green medium-sized bulldozer that had been borrowed from the British contingent, but it appeared to have no armour on it. We needed these vehicles because we were dealing with irrigation ditches, berms and walls made out of heavy clay, as well as thick marijuana fields that needed to be cleared to allow other vehicles to pass. The Zettelmeyer is a very light vehicle that has no business being on the front of an assault. Looking around, I had to wonder if this equipment was adequate for an assault of this magnitude. But it was too late to worry about it now.

Barry, Kash and I jumped into Captain Norton's LAV. It was a tight fit with our massive rucksacks and all our extra sniper equipment. The LAV's rear hull hatches, called air sentry hatches, were open, and two soldiers were sticking out observing what was going on. We pulled out from our position and started our approach towards the white schoolhouse. I was inside the LAV and unable to see out. I was listening on my radio so that I could keep track of what was happening. The original plan was to advance straight towards the schoolhouse, but as we approached, the lead vehicles were swinging to the right on a different path from the one that had been mapped out. It's almost like the lead vehicles were trying to connect to a road instead of clearing a path.

Major Sprague got on the radio. "Okay. Stop. I don't want to go in that direction. I want you to stay away from the main road you're heading towards because it's most likely filled with IEDs and land mines. Stick to the plan we made," he said. "Take your time. Slow down, and let's everybody do this properly."

After that, we were moving slowly but surely. There was the normal banter over the radio as everyone fell in and started following the major's orders.

Up ahead, the first vehicles were closing in on the white schoolhouse. The Zettelmeyer had cleared a way for the lead platoon—comprising four LAVs and a G Wagon—to take a position next to the schoolhouse.

It was at this point that the Taliban decided to make their presence known by firing an anti-tank recoilless rifle round at the softest vehicle of this lead platoon—the G Wagon. The round went right through the front windshield, causing immediate casualties.

Next, our whole assault opened up all at once—every cannon, every coaxial machine gun was firing. Taliban were coming out of the weeds all around us, out of tunnels, windows, mouse holes. They had held their powder to the last second, and then it was game on. They had the defender's advantage, and they used it.

The call went out on the radio that one of our vehicles was hit and we had casualties. As this was happening, one of the LAVs that was next to the schoolhouse went nose-first into a ditch and was stuck. I was trying to listen on the radio when suddenly the troops who were sticking out of the top hatches on our LAV yelled, "Holy fuck, they're right there!" They let go a burst from their C7s, followed by a grenade from a rifle-mounted grenade launcher. It was never the plan for our LAV at the back of the convoy to be engaged like this, but because we'd driven right into an enemy trap, the guys up top had no choice but to defend.

At that moment, our artillery began raining down and air support started dropping bombs on the Taliban. A massive bomb landed right on target but bounced off a couple of buildings and rolled right next to the LAV that was occupied by Major Sprague. I'll never forget hearing Major Sprague over the radio: "What the fuck! Is that a five-hundred-pound bomb that just landed next to *our* vehicle?" Fortunately it didn't detonate, or else Major Sprague and everybody in the vicinity would have been obliterated.

I felt helpless during all of this chaos, because the plan for us as snipers was to get involved only once Objective Rugby had been achieved. At that point, we would get up on the school's roof and provide cover for the bound to the next objective. But in this situation, Barry, Kash and I were stuck inside the LAV right at the time when our shooting skills were needed most up top. I was working the radio, doing my best to keep everyone in the vehicle informed of what was happening up ahead.

"Okay, we've got three WIA and one KIA," I said, relaying the message that there were three wounded soldiers and one who was killed in the G Wagon that had been hit. Every soldier had a "zap number," which was to be used as an identifier in case you were wounded or killed in the field. Standard operating procedure was that if someone died in combat, you never revealed their name during the battle. At this point, we didn't know which soldier had been killed in that attack on the G Wagon. And no one seemed to know the zap number either.

Finally, Major Sprague got on the radio. "I need to know now! Who the fuck just got killed?"

The radio crackled and a voice came on. "It was Warrant Officer Rick Nolan, sir."

Rick Nolan was the soldier I'd had the brief argument with the day before. I have always felt bad that our last conversation was a little strained. Rick was a good man and a great soldier. Sitting in the front seat of that G Wagon, he had no chance of surviving a direct rocket hit.

I looked at Barry and Kash. We were all stunned into silence. No matter how much you prepare for the moment when a soldier you know becomes a casualty, there's nothing that compares to the actual feeling. On top of that, it was jarring for all of us, because we just didn't expect a soldier with his level of experience and status to be the first one taken out on the mission.

Suddenly our LAV accelerated hard and fast. We drove for what seemed quite a distance. We were flying so fast over uneven terrain that we were all getting tossed around. We then slammed to a bone-jarring stop and Captain Norton gave the order to drop ramp. I reached over, flipped the switch and lowered the ramp at the back of our LAV. As snipers, we don't have to wear frag vests or helmets while on missions. We just had our tactical load-bearing gear on us. In hindsight, given the situation, we probably should have been wearing all the protection possible, but we often chose not to.

Once the ramp was dropped, we saw Sergeant Scott Fawcett directing traffic on the ground. With Scott was the driver of the G Wagon that had been hit. He'd been sitting next to Warrant Officer Nolan when he was killed. He was understandably shaken up, his eyes the size of dinner plates. He didn't have a scratch on him.

He turned to me with a look of shock in his eyes and said, "Did you know the windshield of that G Wagon didn't have bulletproof glass?"

I stared at him for a second. I wanted to tell him there's no such thing as bulletproof glass, that some glass is bullet-resistant, but there was nothing on earth that was going to stop anti-tank fire from penetrating a G Wagon. But I kept quiet. All I said was, "Yeah, bro."

Just then, Sergeant Fawcett approached. "We need your help evacuating the wounded," he said. A medic in the back of Rick's G Wagon had been badly injured. Our LAV would transport him to safety. This spot turned into a casualty collection point at the front of the battle. Usually, you want to move your casualties farther back from the edge of fighting and establish a collection point there. But this was a chaotic situation and so we had to improvise.

The back of our LAV was full of all of our sniper gear, so we started rearranging it to make room for wounded personnel. I walked down the ramp to bring the wounded medic into our LAV. I grabbed him under his good arm. His right shoulder was ripped open, a mangled mess. It was so badly damaged I could see his bone. As I walked him up the ramp, from the corner of my eye I saw the interpreter from Rick's G Wagon being led away, his head back, hands held over his face, blood pouring out of his eyes.

"Hey bro," I said to the medic. "We're going to take you to the ambulance." He didn't respond. He groaned and held his shoulder. At that exact moment, a massive explosion went off behind us. The Zettelmeyer was taken out by another round from the Taliban recoilless rifles. These guys clearly knew how to use that weapon, because they were dead-on accurate—in complete contrast to their use of machine guns and rifles. The blast blew me forward and I felt the heat wave across my back. I spun around and saw smoke and dust swirling in the air. In the chaos of combat, time slows down. Every colour, smell and sound becomes heightened. A second feels like a minute. My peripheral vision went from 180 to 340 degrees in that moment.

I saw one of our guys standing amid the dust. He spotted something and had this look on his face like "Holy fuck." He threw his rifle across his back and bent down to pick up a casualty. Those few seconds felt like forever.

I quickly threw the medic into the back of the vehicle on top of all our gear, then we closed the ramp.

"Let's get this guy out of here!" I said to the vehicle commander.

Captain Norton was in contact with other personnel and knew where the new casualty collection point had been set up. But as we were driving back across the moist riverbed and away from the front lines, our LAV got stuck in the sand. This turned out to be a problem for a lot of our LAV vehicles.

The injured medic was sitting with his head down, saying, "Holy fuck! Holy fuck!" over and over. His shoulder was bleeding profusely and he was clearly in a lot of pain. We were sitting around him, me and my two snipers, trying to calm him down. The LAV wasn't going anywhere, despite the driver's attempts to push through. One of the guys up top came down. "We're stuck," he said. "We're not going anywhere."

Upon hearing this, I shrugged, reached up, flicked the switch to lower the ramp, looked at Barry and said, "Are you coming?" Barry knew what I was planning to do. He didn't say a word, just nodded and started out of the vehicle. When we got to the bottom of the ramp, we could see the Bison ambulance and the new casualty collection point a few hundred metres away.

"Kash, you stay back with the vehicle. Barry, you provide cover." I went back into the LAV. "Okay, bro, we're going for a little walk," I said as I put the medic's good arm over my shoulders and grabbed his belt so I could take as much of his weight as possible. "Just don't stop moving your legs," I told him.

"I don't know if I can do this," he said.

"You can do it! I've got you." And with that, we took off running, with Barry leading the way, rifle poised. It was about a three hundred metre sprint to the ambulance. Bullets were flying over our heads and mortar rounds were landing all around. It felt like we were running in slow motion. Every sight I saw was super-HD. My legs were burning but it was inconsequential and I moved through it. The medic on my shoulders was a big guy, but that didn't matter either. I felt his legs moving next to me as he tried to help me carry his weight. Some Afghan National Army soldiers were to my left, some American Humvees on the other side. Vehicles were driving in all directions. As we approached the last hundred metres, the worst of the fighting was behind us.

When we got to the Bison ambulance, it was buttoned up tight. I hammered on the ramp with my rifle. "Open up, open up!" I yelled. "We have one of your own fucking guys here! A medic!"

They lowered the ramp and time sped back up. The medics inside were pretty surprised to see a fellow medic in such bad shape. They took him inside. "Hey man," I told him, "you're with your own now. They'll take care of you." Before leaving, I had one more thing to settle. I couldn't figure out why this ambulance was parked in a way that left the ramp exposed to enemy fire. It made them sitting ducks. I went to the front to talk to the driver. "Why don't you turn this thing around so your armoured side is facing the enemy?"

"Yeah, okay," the driver said with a nod. He turned the vehicle around, which made Barry and me feel a whole lot better.

Then Barry and I stood outside the ambulance, taking a tactical breather. As we watched our own vehicle getting pulled out of the sand, Kash emerged from the chaos, rifle in hand. At first I thought I should be mad since I'd given him orders to stay put, but all I could feel was happy to see him. I knew if it were my team out there, I wouldn't have been able to stay put either.

We weren't sure what to do next, but we sure weren't keen on making a sprint back to our LAV until it was mobile again, so we stayed near the ambulance to secure the area. A few minutes later, another LAV rolled in next to the ambulance. One of the soldiers up top said, "Guys, give us a hand. We've got a KIA with us here." This was my buddy Jeff's unit, but I didn't see Jeff. My stomach sank. "Who's the KIA?" I asked.

"It's Rick. Rick Nolan."

When you're a soldier and you find out your buddy wasn't the one hit, your first thought is "At least it wasn't my buddy," which is what I thought when I heard Rick's name. And a second after thinking that I felt like the worst, most shameful person on earth. I didn't want to ask the question that next popped into my head, but I knew I had to. "Where's Jeff?"

"Oh, he's still out on the objective. He's fine," the soldier told me. I felt relieved and horrible at the same time. I flashed back once more to the last exchange I'd had with Rick.

The ramp was lowered and Barry and I went up. The guys inside were carrying Rick's legs, lifting his body up from the floor. Rick's frag vest had been pulled up in an attempt to cover his severely injured head and face. There was blood everywhere.

I reached down and grabbed Rick under one arm. Barry grabbed the other arm, and we lifted. We'd done casualty collection training dozens of times during simulated drills. During drills, the soldier playing a casualty would tense up his body to make it a little easier for us to carry him. But when Barry and I grabbed Rick, I was struck by how different this was. Rick was hard to carry. He wasn't helping us out. This wasn't a simulation. Rick was dead. We walked Rick to the nearby ambulance and they took him in.

•

The next few minutes are a bit of a blur, but what I remember is that more casualties were arriving, and as a result, Rick's body was moved from inside the ambulance to outside of it to make way for the wounded. Meanwhile, other KIAs were being laid out, so that three soldiers were now lying in a row in plain sight on the ground. It was clear that a lot of soldiers were dealing with the aftermath of our first real battle and the real consequences of seeing friends killed in action.

One of the most important things in the field of battle is taking care of your dead. In fact, the creed of the Royals is "Never leave a Royal behind." On the field, you want to get bodies out of sight as quickly as possible. It's demoralizing for a soldier to witness a dead comrade during battle—especially when it's someone of Rick's stature. I went into the back of a LAV, grabbed a couple of body bags and got to work with some of the other guys. We picked up Rick and zipped him into a bag. One of the other fallen officers was Frank Mellish. For a second, I had a bit of hope, because he was on a stretcher, which meant he might have only been wounded. But once I saw soldiers approach and check his dog tags, I knew he was gone, a casualty of the round that took out the Zettelmeyer. The sad twist was that Frank Mellish and Rick Nolan had been friends for their whole careers, and now they were lying on the ground together. Next, I helped put Private William Cushley into a bag. I'll never forget looking directly into his still-open eyes and saying, "Sorry, bro," as I zipped up his body bag.

While this was happening, Sergeant Major Barnsley was brought over by two other walking wounded, who, despite their own injuries, had gotten the sergeant major to the casualty collection point before taking care of themselves. They sat him down on the ramp of the ambulance. He was bleeding from his ears, obviously concussed, but all he could focus on was his soldiers. He asked me, "How many dead?"

"Three so far," I said, but even as I said it I regretted my words, because he recoiled with a look of anguish as if I'd just smacked him. I'm pretty sure that news hurt him more than any injuries he'd sustained.

I left the sergeant major. Barry and I went back to patrolling around the ambulance. We then noticed that our LAV—the one under Captain Norton's lead—was now unstuck and was pulling away in the distance. Then the ambulance took off with the casualties. The bodies were loaded into another vehicle, and it took off as well. Now it was me, Kash and Barry standing there in the middle of nowhere, with no vehicle. My radio was still in the back of the battle captain's LAV, so I didn't have any direct communication.

The only allies around were a handful of Afghan soldiers in a gully in their unarmoured Fords. They were firing shots towards the enemy force. One guy was firing from his hip, hooting and hollering all the while. But once these fighters realized the Canadian LAVs were retreating, they took off in their trucks, too.

An American soldier trotted up to us. He was bloodied, but it didn't seem to be any of his own blood. He asked me, "Have you seen a helmet anywhere? I went to help a casualty and I put my helmet down. Now I can't find it."

"Sorry, bro, I haven't seen your helmet," I said. I wasn't even wearing my own helmet, so I wasn't overly concerned about his. One of the last vehicles around, an American Humvee, pulled up. He jumped in and it took off before we could even think to stop it.

Barry, Kash and I were now pretty much accidentally stranded. All the Canadian vehicles were gone. We had no ride. We could see the unit gathering in a re-org on the other side of the Arghandab River, about five hundred metres away. If we wanted to catch them, we would have to go on foot across the river basin.

I turned to the guys. "Well, fellas, I guess we're fucking running back." I immediately thought of the movie *Black Hawk Down*, where a bunch of American soldiers run the Mogadishu Mile because their forces left them behind. We were staring down the same predicament ourselves in Afghanistan. We knew that once we crossed the river we were safe, but before that, we were a perfect target for Taliban gunfire.

We started running, with Barry in the lead position and Kash and me trailing behind. I was trying to keep an eye behind us for danger, looking for any signs of enemy activity. A few seconds later, I noticed another Canadian soldier off to the side of our path, standing by himself, staring off into the distance. As I got closer, I saw he had a medical bag over one shoulder and was holding a rifle on the other.

We ran over to him. "Hey bro, what are you doing?" I asked.

The medic was speechless, his eyes glazed and unfocused. I motioned to Barry and Kash. "You two keep going. We'll catch up."

I asked the medic again, "What are you doing? Are you okay?"

"I don't know. I got left behind," he said.

"That's okay," I said. "But you better come with us because I think we're the last ones."

I went to take the medical bag off his shoulder and suddenly he snapped back to life. "Hey—it's okay," he said. "I can haul my own shit."

"Good enough for me," I said, and I pushed him ahead.

We started running back, with some intermittent gunfire spraying around us. My bigger concern was that if we were spotted by the enemy, they would use a mortar or a recoilless rifle to target us. And if they did, it would be game over for us.

As soon as we got to the other side of the riverbed, the shooting behind us stopped. It was almost as if we had crossed an imaginary finish line. We closed on the line of Charles Company's LAVs a couple hundred metres away. They hadn't withdrawn all the way back to our starting position, which had me thinking we were simply regrouping and would shortly recommence the offensive. I expected to hear the sound of our machine-gun turrets re-engaging the enemy or maybe the 25 millimetre firing off a few rounds, signalling we were preparing to assault. But instead, there was an eerie silence as we approached our troops.

We came puffing up to our guys, and I went over to Sergeant Fawcett, who seemed to have taken charge after various men had fallen. "Is there anything we can do?" I asked him.

"Not for now. We're securing this perimeter and that's all I've been told," he said.

"Are we going back today to finish Objective Rugby?" I asked.

"I don't know. I haven't been told anything," he replied.

I turned back to the scene around me. There was a LAV nearby with the ramp down. A handful of soldiers were inside, just staring off into space with vacant expressions. They told me they had to recover the body of a KIA, Sergeant Shane Stachnik. It was a gruesome scene. He was sticking out of his vehicle during combat when an anti-tank round hit. He never stood a chance. One of the soldiers who'd recovered Sergeant Stachnik's body had his trigger finger on his grenade launcher. His buddy was trying to console him, but the guy was sobbing uncontrollably. "It's *not* going to be okay," he cried.

I looked down at the grenade launcher and said, "Is that thing loaded?"

The soldier looked up at me in slow motion. He released his finger from the grenade launcher and opened it up. I was glad to see it was empty. He was in such a state of shock that he hadn't even realized his finger was on the trigger.

"Okay, guys, let's get it together. We're not done. We haven't taken the objective yet, so we're going back in," I said.

I went in search of some senior officers to get a sense of where things stood. Finally, I found Major Sprague.

"We're going to be pulling back now," he said.

Why we wouldn't just pick right up and go back at these guys to reclaim the white schoolhouse was beyond me. We had lost four good soldiers during the fighting, but we had also kicked the enemy's ass and they had suffered at least ten times the number of casualties. We had now "seen the elephant," as the Romans used to say, meaning we knew what to expect in combat, so why wouldn't we carry on the assault? The job wasn't finished. We had aircraft and artillery—two weapons the Taliban fighters didn't. If we pushed ahead fast, we would steamroll them in no time flat. And they wouldn't be expecting it.

But Major Sprague was ordering a full withdrawal to Masum Ghar. We obeyed orders, but it felt like we were going with our tails between our legs. As we were withdrawing, behind us, the white schoolhouse, the cause of so much pain and expenditure, was being levelled by air strikes and artillery until it was a useless pile of rubble.

Major Sprague later called a meeting behind his vehicle of as many troops as he could rally. I found a rock to sit on, and as I was taking a seat, the medic who I'd found dazed in the field came over and shook my hand. He thanked me for pulling him out of there. "Name's JP. Can I sit next to you? I feel like I owe you."

"Don't worry about it, bro," I said. He seemed to feel better sitting next to me, and I kind of felt the same way.

Finally, Major Sprague stood up in front of the group. His mood was sombre. "Fuck this," he said. "We're going back first thing tomorrow morning. We're going to finish this job."

There was a quiet resolve and determination that went through all of us gathered there. These were exactly the words I wanted to hear. We needed to do this for the sake of the men we'd lost. We headed back to our spot on the mountain, where we were to spend the night.

Guns, bombs, bullets, fire, destruction and blood. That was the battlefield we survived that day. I had been training for it since 1994. But it wasn't finished yet. The next morning, we would deal with another set of air strikes—only not in the way we expected.

13

HUNTER-KILLER SNIPER TEAM

THAT NIGHT, none of us slept very well. Tensions were high. American A-10 jets were flying overhead all through the night as they conducted air strikes against the Taliban insurgents in the area. The sound of the A-10 is more like paper ripping than gunfire, and while the noise kept us up, we loved it. It was the sound of punishment raining down on the enemy. Not only were we going back into the battlefield in a few hours, we were also replaying the events of that day in our minds. There was residual shock for all of us, and in the dark as we tried to rest, it was impossible not to feel the invisible damage, the psychological wounds.

It was pre-dawn and I was half awake. Kash was on watch for the final shift of the night. An A-10 burst that sounded much closer than normal brought me fully awake.

I was rubbing my eyes when Kash called down from our observation position. "You're not going to believe this, but I think he just strafed our own guys." Strafing is the technique of firing at ground targets from low-flying planes.

"What the fuck are you talking about?" I said. "Why would—?"

I stopped talking as soon as I looked down to the bottom of the mountain where Charles Company had set up. It was pure chaos. Soldiers were running everywhere and a huge cloud of dust was swirling around the position. Holy shit, Kash was right—it looked like our own guys had been strafed by the A-10. I had a lot of friends down there and I was worried about them. The bullets from the A-10's 30 millimetre Vulcan cannon are like little grenades, and they fire 3000 rounds a minute. A-10 strikes often wipe out everything in their path. I was thankful that our sniper team had decided to go back to our position on the side of the mountain overnight, otherwise we would have been in the line of fire.

I told Barry and Kash to grab their rifles and binoculars and start surveying the area. My fear was that the Taliban fighters had seen what had happened to our unit and perhaps they would try striking while we were vulnerable. From our elevated position, we kept a watch out for danger that lurked in the distance. The JTF guys on the mountain headed to the bottom to help with the casualties. We kept glancing down to see how bad the damage was to Charles Company. We saw one body bag being taken away.

The radio slowly started coming to life and bits of information trickled in. The soldier who was killed was Private Mark Graham, a former Olympic sprinter for Canada. Private Graham had gone out to burn some garbage, which was a standard procedure for getting rid of waste. But just as he lit the fire in his garbage pit, a pair of A-10 aircraft came over the horizon.

At the exact moment Private Graham was starting his garbage fire, the pilots were told in their headset to use the fire they saw as their frame of reference. But that was a different fire, a few hundred metres closer to enemy territory—in fact it was the Zettelmeyer, still burning where it had been struck the day before in the enemy kill zone.

The pilot immediately realized the error and stopped shooting after a second or two, but the A-10 is so fast that by that point it had already fired off about 150 rounds. Private Graham was killed instantly, and dozens of other bullets struck in and around the vehicles and hit sleeping soldiers in their cots.

More than thirty soldiers were injured, and it was an absolute miracle that only one was killed. I later went down to inspect the area. There were bullet holes and pools of blood in between the cots where the troops had been sleeping. If those soldiers had set up their cots a few inches to one side or the other, they would have been killed.

Helicopters began arriving to medevac the injured out of the area, taking them to the base hospital at Kandahar Airfield. The sun was up by now, and the team in the landing zone was popping smoke grenades to mark the landing zone for the helicopters. I was watching one of the Chinook helicopters approach and saw it mistakenly zero on the smoke coming up from the burning Zettelmeyer and head to land directly in the enemy kill zone. I grabbed my radio to tell the pilot not to land there. We all expected RPGs to come flying in from the enemy position at any second and take this thing out of the air. Fortunately, somebody else got word to the helicopter just in time, and the engines went full throttle, shooting the helicopter straight up into the air.

Many of the senior leaders for Charles Company had been wounded in this friendly fire incident, so there was some lingering doubt as to whether our attack would continue as planned. And then, sure enough, the radio announced that Charles Company had been rendered "combat ineffective"—which meant that we no longer had the capability to carry out the ground offensive for Objective Rugby.

The new plan called for Bravo Company to take over the lead offensive role from their spot in the north. Charles Company would stay put. Since Kash, Barry and I were attached to Charles Company as a sniper unit, we had to stay at our location on the side of the mountain rather than head to the battlefield. We remained at our post for the next twenty-one days.

That's not to say there wasn't danger involved. Barry went down the mountain one day to call his wife on the satellite phone. While he was talking, he was shot at by enemy forces and took cover behind some rocks. The Taliban also shot at us with a recoilless rifle, but their rocket fizzled and made it only a tiny way up the mountain.

Our job was to keep watch over the area, and in the meantime, the battle group's new plan had bulldozers ploughing roads in the area to allow access for our heavy vehicles. The problem was that after these roads were bulldozed, the ground underneath became so soft and powdery that it was the perfect base on which the enemy could drop land mines. Ankle-deep in this soft powder, you'd never see the buried land mine until it was too late. The Taliban would drop land mines at night, leaving not even a trace of the explosive to the naked eye.

The JTF sniper team had vacated the area and now a team of Green Berets—U.S. Army Special Forces—took their spot. We were sharing a radio signal with the Green Berets and so one night we got word that a group of them were surrounded by Taliban fighters in a spot called Sperwan Ghar, a place I had never heard of before.

The Green Berets headed out to assist their fellow soldiers at Sperwan Ghar, leaving us alone on the side of the mountain. As they were leaving, they dumped a whole bunch of their extra supplies on us, tossing us batteries, water and rations. We had enough supplies for about thirty guys—even though it was now just Barry, Kash and me.

We were now taking direction from the Americans, who had taken over operational command, and a few days later, we received orders. We would head out to Sperwan Ghar with some members of the Afghan army, where we would assist the Green Berets. At the same time,

I got a radio call from someone at the top of command with Charles Company. "You can't go to Sperwan Ghar with the Americans. You're with us," the officer told me.

"Listen," I said, "you guys are stationary. You don't need us right now. My sniper unit is going to assist the Americans."

"You don't have the authority to do that," he responded.

There was a pause in our conversation while I decided between being diplomatic or telling this guy to straight-up fuck off.

Then a third voice chimed in. It was the American commander, with a message for the leadership at Charles Company. "I'm deploying my assets as I see fit. And right now I have this sniper unit that I need to assist my troops," he said.

Since the Americans had operational jurisdiction, their decision trumped orders from Charles Company. The only way we would be dismissed from this mission was if we got recalled by the Canadian Armed Forces to Patrol Base Wilson . . . and that's exactly what happened that same day.

There, it was decided that our sniper teams would head out on what we called hunter-killer missions to search out insurgents planting land mines and explosives in the roads we were bulldozing. We would do a lot more hunting than killing, but our expertise in reconnaissance and sniping, it was felt, made us the perfect candidates for this initiative. Running these types of missions was fairly unprecedented; in fact, even the JTF guys were surprised we were going to be engaged this way.

•

On one of our first nights out, we went out as a four-man unit—me, Gord, Barry and Kash. When you're working in a small sniper team, your senses become heightened, because you're no longer surrounded by dozens of other soldiers. In a small group, your radar goes on. You can pick up on all kinds of small details that you normally wouldn't. A sniper's ears are his early-warning device. It's not that we all have super hearing (though some snipers do); it's just that we are put into the role of being either the hunter or the hunted. And when that happens, there's a sensory change—a shift in awareness—that happens deep down. The slightest rustle or shift in the air becomes heightened and louder. When you're in the field stalking or doing surveillance, suddenly you can smell things from hundreds of metres away that in any other situation you wouldn't notice. Many times, we snipers could sniff out the enemy long before we saw him. Whether it was the faint whiff of cigarettes, cologne, the smell of diesel fuel or propane from the stove the enemy was using to make their coffee—all these scents that would escape you in regular life became clues to the enemy's presence. Before going out on a sniper mission, I would often stop showering with soap and I'd avoid wearing deodorant. I would wash all my clothes in only plain water, so that I had no artificial scents on me at all. In our ration kits as soldiers, we would get peppermint gum. That gum was one of the first things we snipers got rid of, because the smell was a dead giveaway.

That night, our team headed to where two trails intersected, which looked like a perfect spot to drop a land mine. We had been given orders to shoot Taliban caught doing anything suspicious or in possession of explosives. Gord and I decided to do a stakeout, while Barry and Kash set up about fifty metres away. We had our weapons on our chests and Gord and I were leaning our shoulders against each other, looking out towards the trail ahead. We had our night-vision goggles on and were getting into sniper mode when suddenly Gord let out a muffled yell. I turned to see him swiping at his legs. "What the fuck is going on?" I asked him.

"I think a mouse just went up my leg and sunk its claws into me."

The noise had been loud enough that if there were any Taliban in the area, they were probably alerted to our presence. Barry and Kash got on their radios. "What the fuck are you guys doing over there?"

"Guys," I said. "It's awful. Gord got attacked by a mouse. Call the medevac and bring me a tourniquet!" Gord and I started laughing so hard that we couldn't stop. We still refer to that night as "The Night of the Mouse." And whenever we bring it up, we still howl with laughter.

That wasn't our only close encounter with a rodent during these hunter-killer missions. Another night, we found an enemy casualty collection point. The ground was littered with syringes, because they would pump their fighters full of opium when they were injured in battle. We could tell that Taliban forces were still in the area and a couple of buildings nearby were possible hideouts. We were warned not to go into buildings at night because the enemy often booby-trapped them with explosives. Instead, we decided to get up onto the roof, where we'd have a great perspective of the area.

Just as we settled into our positions, a dog started barking, potentially giving us away. I thought to myself, "Am I going to have to shoot at *another* fucking dog?" Barry, Kash and I debated our next move. We decided against shooting the dog because our gunshots would be too loud. Even with suppressors on our rifles, you could hear them. We were also fairly certain we were going to run into some Taliban fighters, so we wanted to stay as stealth as possible.

A few moments later, I heard some noise just below our position on the rooftop. It sounded like footsteps in the grass. I told Barry and Kash to stay in their positions while I crawled on my stomach to the edge of the roof, where I'd then drop a grenade over on the enemy. I moved as slowly and quietly as possible, with my night-vision goggles providing a good amount of clarity in the pitch-black conditions.

I looked over the edge of the roof expecting to see a Taliban fighter, but I couldn't see anybody. I reached back and grabbed my thermal binoculars to get a better view. Instead of a Taliban fighter in my sights, I saw a bunch of cats chasing mice into a field. These mice were so big their weight bent the tall grasses, creating a loud noise that could easily be mistaken for footsteps.

•

On a different mission as a hunter-killer team, we were stationed inside an empty building near a turn in a road, hoping to catch someone dropping a land mine. We had recruited a couple of machine gunners from Bravo Company because our plan was to stake out this spot for two or three days. As snipers, the longer you're in one place, the higher the chances are the enemy will discover you, so we figured it was best to have a little firepower backup.

As the sun came up on the first morning, I looked outside and noticed a man walking along our path looking down at what I thought were our footprints from the night before. At one point, he stopped, looked up and saw that the footprints led right to our building. He smiled like the cat that just caught the canary. Our Canadian boots left distinctive impressions in the ground. In hindsight, we should have asked that the soles of our boots be imprinted to look like the treads on the sandals of locals. But hindsight is twenty-twenty.

After the strange smile, this man turned around and took the same path back the way he'd come. Now we were wondering, "Is this guy going to come back with some of his Taliban buddies and get into a gunfight with us?" We were definitely on edge.

A couple of hours later, a large group did approach our building— but it was a bunch of kids. Now what were we supposed to do? Had these kids been sent as pawns, or were they just stumbling upon us by accident? One kid was heading straight to the front door. Barry stood on one side of the door, rifle poised, and I stood on the other, with my pistol at the ready. Of course, I wasn't going to shoot an innocent kid or even scare this little guy—he was maybe five or six years old. But if the kid came in, we'd be discovered. And we'd have to do something.

Just as the kid reached for the door handle, his friends called out to him. We watched as his hand slid from the door and he ambled away from the building. We were very relieved that we wouldn't be put in a situation where we had to keep a poor kid hostage for a couple of hours before we could decide how to move forward without being detected.

We spent the next ten days doing this kind of surveillance in various locales, trying to catch the guys dropping the land mines. It was a great way for us to get out in the field and get a better understanding of the situation we were dealing with.

After that, we were assigned back to ISTAR company in early October. They had us holding down an area for a couple of days, then Kash and I returned to Kandahar Airfield to prepare for our extended leaves. My plan was to head to Thailand with my girlfriend at the time. But as soon as I got back to the base, one of the senior officials asked me for some help with a special assignment. This wasn't a mission filled with intrigue and drama. Instead, a handful of senior staff wanted security as they went shopping at a local bazaar.

"Isn't there anybody else to guard you guys while you go shopping?" I asked.

"Nope. Everybody else is busy," the senior officer replied.

I had just come back from a few weeks in the field, where we'd been shot at by enemy troops, watched our fellow soldiers get killed, witnessed our own camp get strafed by friendly fire and packed fallen soldiers into body bags. Now I had to provide protection for a shopping trip? I took the assignment, but I was grumbling under my breath for the whole three hours.

When I returned from the uneventful security duty, someone came running up to me and said, "Your snipers are in some serious shit right now."

"What? My unit?"

"Yes! Your unit."

I grabbed Kash and ran straight to the Tactical Operations Centre, the communications hub. While I'd been babysitting at the bazaar, the Taliban had ambushed ISTAR company. Barry and the rest of our sniper team saw the enemy in advance and alerted everyone about them, but there was no proactive response. The enemy hit our spot with RPGs and killed two soldiers standing next to a vehicle. My sniper team was trapped in a building with Taliban fighters surrounding them, and they needed assistance. Apache helicopters flew in and shot at the enemy, but our snipers couldn't leave with gunfire going off. After the A-10 strafing incident, I think everyone was a little worried about being hit by friendly fire.

"I need to go back out there and rejoin my boys. They need me," I said. But I was told that I had no choice but to go on my scheduled leave. If I had only waited a few more hours, I would have been there to help handle this Taliban ambush. Instead, I was far away and of no help to my fellow snipers. Eventually, they got themselves out of trouble and pushed the Taliban back, but having to listen to this go down on the radio and not being able to help was making me crazy.

Although what happened was completely out of my control, I felt I'd let the team down by not being there. Kash and I saluted as the caskets of the two fallen soldiers from ISTAR were loaded onto the C-130 Hercules that would transport them back home to their grieving families in Canada and down the Highway of Heroes.

At long last, it was time for us to take our planes for our scheduled leaves. Kash and I flew first to Dubai, and the next day I flew to Thailand to meet with my girlfriend.

She and I had met at CFB Gagetown when I was on the master sniper course and we'd been dating for a few months when I was deployed to Afghanistan. I was looking forward to spending three weeks with her. We didn't have much of an itinerary for this trip. We rented a pickup truck and headed to a cleansing resort. These were common in Thailand, and I had always wanted to try one. It wasn't exactly a romantic getaway—the accommodations were simple huts and the cleanse meant going to the bathroom a lot, but after a five-day stay, we both felt a lot better.

During my time in Thailand, I rarely checked my email and tried to unplug from Afghanistan as much as possible. Snipers have the ability to disconnect their emotions, and I think that's what I did in this case. I just turned off. After three weeks, I was ready to get back to work. More than that, I was looking forward to it.

•

Upon my return, I joined our ISTAR unit, which had moved to Sperwan Ghar to assist the Green Beret unit from the United States. Our objective yet again was to push the Taliban out of the area. I arrived at Sperwan Ghar via helicopter, and Gord was waiting for me at the landing zone.

"Good to have you back, man," he said.

"Great to be here," I answered, giving him a huge hug. He showed me around our new home base, which was a police station built out of poured concrete. It was a perfect lookout post, offering great visibility for kilometres in all directions.

ISTAR company had some recce platoon guys, a few artillery soldiers and our sniper team all working to secure the base. A barbed-wire fence separated us from a nearby village. The sniper section kept watch from the top of the water well. (Snipers always prefer to hunker down at the most elevated position.) We worked together to improve the base, building bunkers out of timber, and after that we got pretty comfortable in our surroundings.

Working with the Green Berets was one of the best experiences I had in Afghanistan. I hit it off right away with their commander, a man named Rob. He would call me "Little Brother"—even though I was bigger than he was. I returned the favour by calling him "Big Brother." We had about twenty-five straight days when we were engaged with the Taliban in some fashion. It was like we were fighting them in the Wild Wild West. They had blown up a Green Beret vehicle with a land mine, destroying it and angering a lot of the American guys stationed at Sperwan Ghar. At the start of the mission, our sniper team was only helping in a secondary role. We were the eyes and ears for the team, serving as the lookout. It was our job to call in the artillery air strikes, and we were doing that on a daily basis. We kept a list of all the NATO aircraft that we had called in and we managed to use almost every type of aircraft in the NATO inventory, from a Predator drone to a B-2 stealth bomber.

Of course, we wanted to have our roles increased and were hoping to use our actual sniper skills in the field alongside the Green Berets. But our chain of command was continually resisting our involvement; our ISTAR commander repeatedly said he didn't want us out there. "This isn't part of our mandate" was the standard answer we received. Regardless, I hung out with the Green Berets and pestered them to let us join. I wanted to be engaged in the battle so badly it was making me sick. And I would get even more nauseous watching the Green Berets asking our chain of command for our help—only to be rejected each time.

Finally, after a couple of weeks of unrelenting pressure, our chain of command allowed the recce platoon to head out in their LAVs and support the Green Berets on one of their missions. Though they'd had some contact with the enemy, there were no casualties or damage from the engagement, and that seemed to open up the door to our involvement. A few days later, the Green Berets went on an early-morning ambush of a known Taliban route next to a river. Big Brother

Rob said, "I'm going to have sniper support on this mission." And with that, we had our first mission.

It was determined that I would go out with a fellow sniper, Yves, whose nickname was "B." B had the reputation of being a ninja—so calm and stealthy that he could sneak up on anybody. The plan called for the Green Berets to lay some Claymore anti-personnel mines next to the path where we thought the Taliban were going to be walking. Claymore mines contain thousands of ball bearings that release out in a fan once detonated.

B and I set up for the ambush; B was on the top of a narrow grape-drying hut, and I stayed on the ground next to it. We travelled light, B bringing his sniper rifle and a couple hundred rounds of ammo while I brought a C8 with a suppressor, some water and the radio. I had gotten into the habit of not wearing my Kevlar helmet, so I actually went out wearing a ball cap with a Canadian flag Velcro'd onto it. Two Afghan National Army soldiers were assigned to be our security. One of them at some point said to me, "When we catch an Arab, we cut off his head."

I was sort of taken aback. "Um. That's not really something I can be a part of. But it's your country. You can defend it any way you want."

These ANA guys were thirsty for revenge because they'd lost their sergeant major a few days earlier when their convoy tripped a road-side bomb. The Green Beret team was pretty aggressive, too; they had already moved forward and were planting the Claymore mines in the ground. Their most experienced guy was a man they nicknamed Silverback for his grey hair and a gorilla-like build. He'd already planted many mines, and we were expecting the Taliban to cross the area in about forty minutes.

As I've often learned on the battlefield, nothing ever goes according to plan. While Silverback was out there planting the mines, he looked up and suddenly found himself face-to-face with a pair of Taliban soldiers. The three of them stared at each other in a tense stand-off, waiting to see who was going to blink first.

Suddenly Silverback yelled, "Blow them!"—giving the order to detonate the mines—and dove backwards to safety. The two Taliban fighters never stood a chance. They were killed instantly.

A few minutes later, about forty Taliban fighters came across the river to our position. I looked around and realized that our ANA security team—the two guys who were hell-bent on revenge—had disappeared. During the chaos of the Claymore mine explosion, they just took off.

The Taliban fighters were advancing. B and I saw they had us surrounded in a horseshoe formation. This had gone from an ambush on the Taliban to a battle where we'd be lucky to get out alive. We knew that we had to shoot our way out using the opening in the horseshoe.

We began shooting, but Rob was determined that with this turn of events we should turn around and start chasing the Taliban back. So for the next three hours, we engaged with the Taliban to beat them back. B was pissed with me because he didn't have his C8; I'd told him that all he needed was his sniper rifle.

I must say that the Taliban put up a hell of a fight. One of their fighters jumped out of a building wielding an RPG and fired that sucker right at a Green Beret. And just like in the movies, the American was able to duck at the last second and avoid the lethal shot. He looked over at his buddy and said, "Did that son of a bitch just fire an RPG at me?"

His buddy said, "Yep."

"Well, fuck him." And this American guy jumped up off the ground, dusted himself off, went into that building with a gun and took out all the Taliban fighters in there. I was back watching all this unfold with my mouth hanging open thinking to myself, "Holy crap. That is badass!"

I took out a Taliban fighter who was about a hundred metres away, though a Green Beret who also had the same guy lined up says the kill was his. In the end, we just agreed that we both took him out.

I then went looking for B, who I found on a roof. He was positioned in the low part between two of the five peaks. I came under pretty accurate enemy fire and started jumping from peak to peak. I could hear bullets whizzing past me. I was clearly in the line of sight of some enemy fighter, and they had me dialed in. I got to B and tucked myself into the next low spot to his.

In the distance, I located the guy who'd been shooting at me; he was behind a huge mound of dirt about 150 metres away. I was trying to give the coordinates to B, but every time I poked my head up, a few rounds would ricochet around us and I was so amped up I was stammering.

He looked at me and said, "What the fuck are you talking about? I'm busy!"

Unbeknownst to me, B had several other enemies in his sights about 500 metres away and without any help had already sent two of them to paradise before I found him. He would later receive a commendation for his actions that day.

I ended up taking the shot myself instead of trying to spot for B. I'm positive my bullet was the one that killed the guy, though once again, a Green Beret believed it was his.

At this point, we got the command over the radio to start pulling back. We had forced the Taliban to retreat and our ammo supplies were starting to run low. As I was leaving the area, I noticed something out of the corner of my eye. It almost looked like a football dropping from the sky. I would later learn that it was a 250-pound bomb called in by the JDAM—joint direct attack munition—to cover our retreat. And one of these calls was aimed for the building right next door.

When the bomb landed, the force of the explosion knocked me right off my feet and against a wall. And I'll never forget how the window next to me shattered and a couple of dishrags came flying out—right in front of my face.

The recce platoon picked us up in their LAVs and took us back to Sperwan Ghar. We did our debriefing meeting and estimated that we had killed between thirty and forty Taliban fighters. But as the meeting was concluding, someone tapped me on the shoulder and said, "Jody, you're going back to Kandahar." And just like that, I was reassigned. I didn't want to go, but personnel switches like this were often made to keep people fresh.

●

I spent a couple of days back at Kandahar Airfield, doing my laundry, showering and getting all my stuff back in order. But I was itching to return to Sperwan Ghar—especially since we now had approval to do some further work with the Green Berets.

After just a few days, I got word that I could return.

I arrived in the middle of a commotion. Kash was lined up behind a sniper rifle and some Green Berets were there, too. "What's going on?" I asked.

"We have a Taliban guy laying an IED on the road to the west," one of the Green Berets told me.

I hadn't even put my gear away, and here I was, back in the action. I picked up a pair of binoculars and spotted a lone guy in the distance standing next to his camel.

"Glad you're here, bro," Kash said. "Help me get a read on this guy. I'm trying to figure out the distance."

Kash and I had always had a great rapport, and I was thrilled to be coaching him through this. "Okay—put eighteen hundred into your scope," I said. "The target appears to be standing about eighteen hundred metres away."

Kash took his shot and we saw a puff of dust off a wall, but the Taliban guy didn't even flinch, so we knew we had missed by a healthy margin.

"All right, Kash—let's do fourteen fifty on the scope," I said. I knew that our target was a small window—basically only the waist up on this guy. Kash shot again, and this time the bullet skipped across a couple of walls. But the guy definitely heard the bullet this time. He looked around, but wasn't bothered and continued his work.

"Last range I've got, Kash, is sixteen fifty. Let's try that." At this point, time seemed to slow down. Each heartbeat felt like it lasted a minute. Kash took a deep breath and pulled the trigger. Two seconds later, the guy fell over like a sack of potatoes. We wanted to investigate and confirm the kill ourselves, but our chain of command thought otherwise—as usual. They were going to send an airplane in for the confirmation. As this was happening, we noticed a man walking with a camel and a donkey. We weren't too suspicious of him, but he was getting closer to the spot where we'd made our hit.

I watched as a look of terror and panic came over him when he realized the man on the ground was dead. He quickly started to walk away with his animals, but then he abruptly stopped and did a 180-degree turn. He came right back and grabbed at the tether on the dead guy's camel and took it along with him. We'd killed a Taliban fighter, and this guy walked away with a free camel.

That wasn't the only instance when someone ended up with free animals during my time at Sperwan Ghar. Once, we were headed out on an ambush mission with the Green Berets. There were three of us snipers in total and we had set up the perfect view of the kill zone. The only problem was that a herd of donkeys wandered into the area and showed up at that exact spot. The Taliban never arrived, so these donkeys were the central attraction. They even followed us all the way back to our base—although we didn't let them through the main security gate. They stayed out there and made this their new home. A few of the ANA soldiers actually ended up using them as pack animals to cart gear around.

During the course of a war, tragedy looms large, but humour keeps everybody grounded. When we were at Sperwan Ghar, for example, we were getting big care packages sent to us by Canadians back home, friends and family, of course, but also from strangers. These would contain all sorts of things. Sometimes they were treats for us—like Snickers bars or candy canes; other times we would get items that people were hoping would be passed along to the less fortunate in Afghanistan. For example, we once received a massive box filled with kids' toothbrushes. These were sent with the expectation that we would hand them out to local children. Problem was, we never ran into any kids at Sperwan Ghar. It was a very isolated position. We ended up using the toothbrushes ourselves, sometimes using two or three a day. After all, we needed to keep up with our oral hygiene given the number of sugary treats coming our way.

My sister, Katie, used to send me homemade cookies that I absolutely loved. The problem was, all the other soldiers liked her cookies, too, and would often try to sneak some from my stash. One time, I was keeping watch over an area. A company commander sitting next to me decided to help himself to a bag of Katie's cookies I'd left on a nearby table. He had a heaping handful and there were crumbs everywhere.

I wanted to say, "What the fuck are you doing with my cookies, man?"—but he was one of my superiors, so I couldn't mouth off to him. Instead, I grabbed the bag off the table and hid it. I think he got the message. That was the last time I ever left Katie's cookies out on a table—or anything else around that guy.

Getting care packages from friends and family always reminded me of home. I was fortunate enough to get to use a satellite phone to connect with family and friends from time to time, but things didn't always go smoothly during those conversations.

One time I was on the satellite phone with my dad when a bullet went whizzing over my head. This was bizarre because it was in the middle of the afternoon in broad daylight.

"Um, Dad, I'm going to have to let you go," I said.

"Why? What's wrong?" he asked.

"Oh, nothing. Don't worry about it. There's just something I have to do," I said calmly. I certainly didn't want my dad worrying.

While Kash had a kill at 1650 metres, during those twenty-five days at Sperwan Ghar I had a chance to break the record for the longest kill. The Green Berets were in contact with the enemy forces, who were within the range of our .50-calibre sniper rifle. I was eager to lend some assistance. I wasn't a huge fan of the .50-calibre because I never liked the ammunition. But I wanted to jump into this situation, so I took the rifle, and Gord came along to spot for me.

The range was pretty extreme: Gord measured the enemy target and estimated it was around 2500 metres away. We were excited because this was just over Rob Furlong's record of a kill at 2430 metres. We could actually break the record if we executed this to perfection.

We took off the suppressor to give the rifle maximum range. At 2500 metres, your bull's-eye is only about two feet across in any direction. It's not exactly pinpoint accuracy at a range like that. I squeezed the trigger, but I missed my first target by four to ten feet. But even worse was the fact that I'd forgotten to put my earplugs in. The sound was absolutely deafening, like a grenade going off right next to my head. I took a few more shots, but each time, my hearing got worse and worse. Somebody tossed me some earplugs, but at that point it was too late. I had ringing in my ears for about four years afterwards.

And to make matters worse, I came so close to making the longest kill, only to come up short. But as they say, close only counts in horse-shoes and hand grenades.

•

In early December, we got orders for Operation Baaz Tsuka, a mission to push the Taliban out of the remaining villages in the Panjwaii district and around Sperwan Ghar. The Green Berets led the operation with considerable assistance from the Canadians and members of the ANA. The plan was for us to make it to a place called Zangabad Ghar, which was a massive rocky hill. It was about three and a half kilometres away from Sperwan Ghar, but the path was riddled with Taliban hot spots. And since we had been in contact with them on so many occasions over the previous weeks, we were prepared for a significant battle. We assumed it would take us at least a full day just to make it halfway to our destination.

As it turned out, the Taliban didn't want to fight, and we encountered very little resistance. In fact, it was extremely uneventful for us getting to the hill. The Green Berets had our sniper team move up to a high point, and they wanted us to call in a couple of artillery strikes about four hundred metres ahead, on top of Zangabad, so they could move freely once they arrived.

I accidentally called in the strike too long, but it did hit a target. The enemy chatter picked up over the radio. Our intelligence intercepted their messages and our interpreters confirmed the hit on their hidden position. The interpreters heard the enemy force saying, "How did they find our location?"

I immediately called for another strike in the exact same location. "Repeat!" I yelled into my radio, and we made another direct hit on the enemy's hideout. We definitely disrupted their plan, and they scurried away. With them out of the area, we easily moved into our position at the top of the hill. As soon as we settled into our spot, we spotted a Taliban fighter in a grove of trees. He was walking around with a gun, so he was fair game for us. Finally, he sat down, and just his head was visible.

I debated taking the shot. I was able to shoot a pop can at about a thousand metres, so this distance was good for me, but Kash was the one currently holding the rifle and I didn't want to take the chance away from him. Instead, I served as his spotter. As we were getting ready to take a shot at this guy, we were suddenly surrounded by the Green Berets, who became interested spectators. "Oh, man, this is going to be good!" Some of them grabbed binoculars and were taking bets as to whether Kash could hit his target.

I coached Kash through the motions, told him to take a deep breath and instructed him to fire. He pulled the trigger and we all watched in anticipation. A puff of dust came up from a wall just in front of the Taliban fighter. Kash had aimed slightly low and had missed the guy. The Taliban fighter was stunned and promptly fled.

Of course, there was no end to the ribbing we took from the Green Berets for missing our target. "I guess that's what happens when you get a Canadian to do an American's job," one of them quipped.

We reminded them that it was a Canadian sniper who held the record for the longest kill, so us Canucks were every bit as good as the Americans.

It was certainly a tad embarrassing that we missed this guy by a couple of inches, but the Americans had their share of embarrassing moments as well. While we were in the middle of Operation Baaz Tsuka, I suddenly heard the distinctive sound of *The A-Team* theme song playing in the distance. Sure enough, a Green Beret unit was blaring the tune from their loudspeakers as their Humvee rolled in. Even the other Green Berets around were red in the face.

•

On our first night at Zangabad, the sun was setting to the west of us and was directly in our eyes. It was sort of blinding us. I was starting to take off my gear for the night when suddenly I heard a loud *pop, pop, pop*. I looked up to see tiny footballs flying over our heads. "Holy shit—RPGs!" someone yelled. Then we heard machine-gun fire in front of us and to both sides. The Taliban had initiated another horse-shoe ambush attack and they had smartly waited until the setting sun was in our eyes. They knew the terrain and the way the light could wreak havoc on us. Fortunately, they weren't too accurate with their RPGs, which went about a hundred metres over our heads, causing little damage.

I threw my frag vest back on and picked up a rifle. Barry and Kash were lying on their stomachs with their sniper rifles. I instructed Barry to use the GPS to get a range on these guys and figure out where the RPGs were coming from. As soon as he got the coordinates, I called in the grid to the JTAC, who were in charge of the air strikes in the area. Less than two minutes later, we had aircraft dropping bombs on them. As quickly as their ambush started, it was shut down by our air-craft. Fortunately, none of our guys ended up getting hurt, although we considered ourselves pretty lucky.

The aircraft support was critical in these types of situations. An-other time, a couple of A-10 jets helped us out of a jam when we were surrounded by Taliban fighters. The NATO commander, who was a Dutch general, had asked for a huge amount of cover and protec-tion because he had a meeting in a nearby village. But by the time we reached the village, all of the NATO units were pulling out because the commander's meeting was over. As the coalition forces were leav-ing, the Taliban fighters were increasing in numbers. The next thing we knew, we were the only coalition call sign in the area. And Taliban fighters started coming towards us. We weren't in armoured vehicles but on ATVs, so we called in some air support. The A-10s flew right in, flying a figure-eight pattern overhead to make sure we got out safely. A couple of days later, when we pulled into Patrol Base Wilson, the regimental sergeant major was upset that we were riding in ATVs while the rest of the convoy was in LAVs and Coyotes. The RSM told us, "You guys are never riding those ATVs again, because there is zero protection from mines." That was fine by us.

We then stayed at Patrol Base Wilson to help on another mission. We set up three bases in the Panjwaii valley—Strong Point North, South and Centre. The problem with our so-called strong points was that the enemy was constantly attacking them. Eventually, our commanding officer decided enough was enough. He asked us snipers to find the attackers.

We set out in a six-man sniper unit to hunt these guys down. We found the spot where they were coordinating their attacks and reported our findings back to the commanding officer. A few nights later—on New Year's Eve—we were sent in the same six-man sniper unit for a reconnaissance mission. Gord was the patrol leader, and I was the second-in-command. Barry and Kash joined us, alongside two others.

This was a mission that was done under the cloak of darkness, except we encountered a problem. Our troops fired off a bunch of para-flares and rounds to ring in the New Year. We had to run for cover from our own guys in case one of these celebratory rounds accidentally went off near us.

After midnight, calm finally reigned, and the six of us headed out with our night-vision goggles. We formed a line, with me bringing up the rear. We travelled a path, keeping the usual ten metres between us. Suddenly our line came to a screeching halt. Barry had spotted something up ahead. He was talking with Gord at the front, so I broke our formation to find out what was going on.

"Check that out," Barry said. A wall along the path had partially collapsed, a major red flag. This is often the sign of a booby-trapped area or an impending ambush. We weren't too concerned about an ambush, because the Taliban didn't often attack that late unless they had large numbers of fighters. And the area was fairly quiet, so we didn't think an attack was imminent. Still, there were very good odds that land mines or IEDs were planted in the ground near this path, so now we had to take a moment to figure out the best way forward.

We huddled in a 360-degree formation, with all six of us pointing our weapons outwards. After a few minutes, Barry went forward on his own to get a better read on the area.

When he returned, he said, "Turn around and follow the exact same footprints we used to get into this area. We are in the middle of a fucking minefield."

Sure enough, we could see all kinds of odd debris on the ground. Were they land mines? We couldn't be sure, but we were sure of one thing: we didn't want to step on one to find out the answer. We turned around and marched back in a straight line, following in our own footsteps.

We got out of the area safely and spent the night at a nearby base. As the sun rose, we returned to the path to get a better look in the daylight. We retraced our steps to where we'd been the night before and found ourselves standing not in a minefield but amongst the wreckage of a missile, a smashed cellphone, pieces of an AK-47 and some body parts. Now everything made sense. A few days earlier, a Predator drone had dropped a missile in that area at the same time that a Taliban fighter was dropping land mines.

Everything changes in the light of day, and we now knew our mission could proceed. We continued to the small village ahead. The plan was for us to check on enemy movement and report back to Alpha Company, which we were supporting.

In the distance, we scoped out a small clutch of houses that were connected by some mud walls. Our plan was to get up onto the roof of one of them. As luck would have it, we chose the one compound that wasn't occupied. We would later learn that all the other units had families living in them.

When we were up on the roof, I radioed back to Alpha Company with our position.

"Can you repeat your coordinates?" the officer on the other end asked. He couldn't believe that we'd made it that deep into enemy territory. They were at least four kilometres behind us, so we knew we'd be on our own for a while. The Alpha Company commander did not report our position to any of his higher-ups for fear of getting in trouble.

We tried to stay out of sight, especially from local teenagers. These teens often patrolled in groups of two or three and then reported back to Taliban leaders about what they saw. They were never armed, because they knew we would shoot anybody we saw carrying a weapon. This technique reminded me of the way gangs in North America use younger kids to do their dirty work.

A couple of these teenagers circled our compound. We could see them, but they couldn't see us . . . yet. If they spotted us, we'd have a full firefight on our hands, with no backup support. The kids pulled on the front door of the compound, but it was sealed shut. There was a side door with a flimsy lock, and if these kids tried that door, they would get in with little problem. Gord and I quickly went downstairs to secure the side door. I pulled out my pistol. What was I going to do if I came face-to-face with a teen spying for the Taliban? Would I shoot the kid, even though he was unarmed? Would I take him hostage? Here I was again, wondering how the hell to deal with children caught up in the mess of war and hoping I would not have to act.

As Gord stood guard, his rifle in the ready position, I pressed myself against the door, putting all my weight against it. If one of these kids tried the door, he would meet some resistance. Hopefully that would be enough for him to give up. As I leaned back, I looked over at Gord. He shook his head. "This is out of a fucking movie," he said.

And it was. It was so surreal that we couldn't help but laugh. It's not that we weren't aware of how serious the situation was, but sometimes, all you can do in the face of danger is laugh. So we did. Uncontrollably.

"Fuck off," I whispered to Gord. "Stop fucking laughing."

What finally made us snap out of it was peeking through tiny holes in the door, where we saw how close these kids were to us.

One of the teenagers approached the door, reached for the handle and pushed. Just then, one of his buddies yelled something to him and the kid took off.

We watched them run away down a path. Once they were at a safe distance, Gord and I exhaled. Then we started to laugh again, this time even harder.

We waited in that stakeout position for a couple more hours, but then word came over the radio that we were to leave—immediately. One of the tanks in the battle group had hit a land mine on its way over and now the whole unit was swinging its line of advance and changing its approach. But how were we supposed to leave at one o'clock in the afternoon, a six-man unit walking in broad daylight? We always tried to move under the cover of darkness, plus the teenage lookouts were still somewhere in the area.

But we had orders, so we followed them. As soon as we opened the door, we came face-to-face with those same teenagers. We locked eyes, and then they took off in the other direction.

"Off to tell the Taliban fighters or off to tell Mom?" I asked the guys.

"Either way, let's not find out," Kash said.

"Roger that," I replied. "Let's hustle." Afghan women had a reputation for being fierce defenders of their children, a reputation that went all the way back to Alexander the Great. I didn't want to be the soldier Junior pointed out.

And with that, we started the long daylight march back to our base. Fortunately, we didn't encounter any enemy fighters on our way out.

•

Those twenty-five days of engagement with the Taliban and the weeks after were tense and tough, but also some of the most exciting times I've had in the military. In between all these missions, we would go to one or another of the Strong Point bases to rest and unwind. Because we were a roving sniper unit, we often didn't have set accommodations or an area that we could call our own. All the time we were in Sperwan Ghar, we passed the time by watching *Super Troopers*. We must have watched that movie about two hundred times. And I have watched it two hundred times since then.

The ambulance crews usually had some extra space, so we often spent time with them. One of the medics, a woman named Alannah, always made sure we felt welcome in their area. Alannah would set up her portable DVD player and the two of us would sit there and watch endless episodes of *Family Guy*, which was a great way to pass the time and relax. I found I had a great connection and chemistry with her, but of course, fraternizing within the Armed Forces is strictly forbidden. And besides, I knew that she was married to a guy who used to be in a battalion with us, so she was off-limits in more ways than one. I was also still in a long-distance relationship with my girlfriend back home, so I figured this relationship with Alannah would be nothing more than platonic. But while we were watching *Family Guy* one night, she leaned closer to me and casually mentioned that she and her husband were separated.

"That's too bad, I'm sorry to hear that," I said. We left it at that, but I do remember wondering if our paths would somehow cross down the road. As it happened, our paths didn't only cross, they converged. Just a few days later, Alannah would play a critical role in saving my life.

PART
4

The ultimate wound is the one that makes you miss the war you got it in.

—Sebastian Junger, *The Perfect Storm*

14

FINAL STEPS

IN EARLY December of 2006, I had a strange experience while standing atop our position at Sperwan Ghar. Suddenly I was overwhelmed with a feeling of dread—like something bad was going to happen to me. I'd never experienced a sixth sense like that before, and I have never had it since.

On January 11, one week after my thirtieth birthday, we were sent on a new mission. Our battle group was doing a "soft knock" to flush out Taliban, which meant arriving out of the blue at an Afghan village. As snipers we were asked to support it. Just like when cops arrive unannounced at a criminal's door, we hoped our appearance would startle the enemy into peaceful surrender.

We were a four-man sniper unit on this mission—me, Barry, Kash and Gord. The plan was to leave from the Strong Point Centre location at 3:30 a.m. so that we could be in our sniper positions ready to infiltrate the village at the first sign of daylight. I packed up my ruck-sack, but since I was now a veteran in the field, I no longer loaded it down with a hundred pounds of equipment the way I had in the early days of the tour. Now I carried only the essentials—two bottles of water, a granola bar, some spare batteries, my radio and as much ammo as I could carry. The radio was how we communicated with our operations base. There was only one, and it was my job to carry it. It was the heaviest item we had.

We stepped outside the wire at Strong Point Centre past a landmark called "the ant hill" and skirted the cemetery that always creeped me out because of the negative energy I felt when we were near it. A lot of violent death happened in this area and many lain to rest were Taliban fighters we'd put there. We changed direction and headed through the thick mud of a large farmer's field. A few minutes later, we arrived at an opening in a wall leading into the village we wanted to observe. This entry seemed like an easy way in. But as any good sniper knows, obvious entry points are often traps. Snipers are trained to find an unconventional approach, to search out the road less travelled, because the road less travelled is always the safest.

I was bringing up the rear in our four-man unit, and I couldn't see what was up ahead. Barry—who was always razor-sharp—scanned the area using night-vision goggles and the infrared laser on his rifle. He indicated that the coast was clear, and when Barry said that, it was always a relief.

Two small steps led up to the low entry. Barry took them first, then ducked his head and cleared the doorway. He nodded once on the other side—no issues. He stood guard there, scanning the dark with his night-vision, making sure there was no imminent threat. Gord, Kash and I waited. We were perfectly still and quiet. All snipers are very good at stillness.

Barry gave the signal and ushered first Gord and then Kash through the opening. They were clear. I was the last one left to go through. Kash went down on one knee and pointed his rifle at six o'clock while Gord and Barry manned twelve o'clock and nine o'clock respectively. They had my back. I was ready to go. I took the two steps up and cleared the entry without any problem. I tapped Kash on the shoulder to let him know I was through. He started to walk, and I waited, covering our six while the others moved ahead. Another rule of soldiering, tactical spacing—never bunch up.

Once he was about ten metres ahead, I turned and took my first step forward. My right foot touched the ground, and a massive orange fireball soared across my face. I didn't hear a sound. For a few seconds, I felt weightless, as if I was suspended in space.

The next thing I knew, I was on the ground. My ears, nose and mouth tasted like mud. And that's when the pain hit, a pain so intense that it completely overwhelmed my body and my silence. I started punching the ground and screaming, "Oh my god! Oh my god!" It was the only time in my life I'd ever uttered anything religious.

The blast was so powerful it had knocked Kash down, and I saw him in the dirt up ahead of me. For a few seconds, I couldn't see Barry or Gord. They had probably done what good snipers are supposed to do upon hearing an explosion: run for cover and prepare for an ambush. A few seconds later, once they realized what had happened, they came running back towards me.

It's such a small thing, a land mine—about the size of a hockey puck but twice as thick, and full of explosives. It was a freak accident, that step I took. Barry, Gord and Kash had all walked over the same spot, but by chance, they missed the device. Or maybe they grazed it but didn't set it off. I was the heaviest soldier in our group, especially when carrying the radio, and that may have had something to do with my setting it off. I was the last in line that day, which was a good thing, because beneath the land mine was a mortar round with shrapnel that, whether by accident or design, would have taken the head off anyone walking behind me.

My mates were all around me now. They hadn't been hit. I stared up at them, but I couldn't move. "Sorry, guys, I just fucked the mission."

Barry crouched over me. "Don't worry about it, man," he said. He began first aid while Gord took the radio from my rucksack to call in the 9liner (medical evacuation).

It was dark and my eyes were full of dirt. I tried to look down at my legs, but I couldn't see the extent of my wounds. The pain in my right leg was excruciating. I grabbed a tourniquet from my shoulder strap and thrust it into Barry's hand. "Man, aren't you going to tourniquet my leg?"

"Sure. Sure I am," Barry said. He started wrapping up my legs.

"Barry," I said. "Just tell me one thing. Are my cock and balls okay?"

"Yeah, man. You're good." I reached down with my hand and did a quick inspection and he laughed.

"My job right now is to survive," I told myself. "If you go into shock, Mitic, you're fucking dead." I concentrated on controlling my breathing, keeping my heart rate steady and remaining conscious.

As Barry dealt with my injuries, Kash kept his eye out for signs of danger. Knowing Kash, he was probably playing out all the worst scenarios in his mind and planning what to do for each one. Gord was on the radio and doing his best to give our coordinates and explain the severity of the situation.

As much as I was trying to stay cool and calm, I was growing more and more concerned about our isolated location. How could a medevac ambulance get through the treacherous terrain? And there wasn't a helicopter landing zone for miles. We were in big trouble.

The next hour was the longest of my life. I was in absolute agony and trying my hardest to stay positive. I was also trying hard not to think about the possibility of bleeding out. Your mind can go to the weirdest places in situations like that. I was starting to get dehydrated, so every few minutes I would have Barry pour just a little bit of water into my mouth, but not too much. I remembered an episode of *M*A*S*H* where Hawkeye says it's a bad idea for the wounded to chug water, and for some reason, in that moment I chose to take my medical advice from a TV show that had been off the air for decades.

With each passing minute, I was growing weaker and weaker. Every time I closed my eyes, it was harder to open them again. I knew that if I lost consciousness, it was over.

Barry and Gord were standing over me. "Do you think I'm going to make it?" I asked Gord.

"Of course you're going to make it. Never give up, bro. You know that." He was saying what I needed to hear, and I had no choice but to believe him. I couldn't help thinking of TCCC—Tactical Combat Casualty Care. This course trains infantry soldiers to do more detailed first aid until a medic arrives on the scene and to assist the medic once he or she arrives. None of us had taken that course. But what we did have was four experienced soldiers in a bad situation together. I trusted the guys to look after me. And we all trusted the system to get us out of there.

A while later, in the distance I could hear the engine of a LAV. So Gord hadn't been lying. Help was close by. But whoever the help was, they would have to make their way on foot for a few hundred metres because there was no way a vehicle could get through the terrain.

I heard some voices coming from the other direction, and soon enough, some guys from the recce platoon were at our side. As it turns out, after Gord radioed our coordinates, the recce platoon— which was about a kilometre away—didn't even wait for orders. They just ran our way, a fact that speaks volumes about the kinship between snipers and recce units.

Jamie, a recce medic, quickly assessed my situation. "We need to stop the blood loss. Fast," he said. He and one of his men took out more tourniquets and applied them to my legs. One was wrapped so tightly that the handle broke. When they were done, I had three tourniquets on each leg.

"How you holding up, buddy?" Jamie asked.

"I'm in fucking agony, man."

Jamie gave me a shot of morphine right away. I'd never been given morphine before, and I assumed it would be just like in the movies, when relief floods through the body the second the syringe is plunged. But nothing changed for me.

"It's not working."

"Bro, it takes fifteen to twenty minutes to kick in."

"Are you fucking kidding me? Give me another shot right now!"

"I'm not sure that's a good idea," said Jamie.

"Just give it to me! Because if you don't give it to me and I live through this, I'm going to kick your ass."

Against his better judgment, Jamie relented. He later confessed that he gave me the second dose because he didn't think I was going to make it anyhow, so what difference did it make?

Jamie now turned for another look at the lower half of my body. He gave me the first real assessment of the damage. "Jody, one of your feet is gone, but the other one might be okay," he said.

I heard a female voice bark out, "What's going on there? Give me an update." It was a familiar voice, but at that moment I couldn't quite place it.

"It's all good," the leader of the recce platoon responded. "Our medic has it under control."

"That's great," the voice fired back. "But *I'm* the medic in charge, so I need an update."

I couldn't take it any longer. "Hey, do you think we can stop the arguing and just worry about saving my life?"

The pain was still excruciating. Gord was wearing a headlamp with a red lens on it. We all wore them when we needed light but also needed to stay tactical. To keep myself focused, I stared at that lens on his forehead. I was feeling myself falling away from everything, from all the red lights around, and I just needed to focus on something brighter, so I reached up and flicked the filter off Gord's headlamp. Now, it shone bright white light in my eyes. That threw a few people off, because bright light can give away your position, but Gord realized what I was doing, and he never left my side.

A few minutes later, a Badger armoured engineering vehicle showed up with a Bison ambulance right behind it. At this point, we had fifty or so troops on the scene.

"Wow," I said. "A lot of people came to my party."

No one laughed.

I was put onto a stretcher and loaded into the back of the ambulance. A few seconds later, the lead medic I'd heard earlier popped her head in and said, "All right, so who do we have here?"

And that's when I saw Alannah—Alannah, my new friend and colleague, the one who watched *Family Guy* with me to pass the time.

Alannah had been so focused on setting up the evacuation plan that she hadn't even known who the injured soldier was—until now. Her face fell the second she saw me.

"Oh, Jody!" she gasped. "I didn't expect to see you here."

"Well, I never expected it either," I said.

As the Bison ambulance started to drive away, she put an IV into my arm. I could hear helicopter propellers in the distance—an American Black Hawk medevac chopper would take me from Masum Ghar to the Kandahar Airfield. At the end of the fifteen-minute ambulance ride, Alannah said, "Okay, Jody. We're putting you in the helicopter now, and I want to see you again. You hear me?"

I was so weak by this point and still in so much pain that the best I could do was nod.

The next thing I remember, I was in the medevac helicopter and an

American medic was hooking my IV line into a saline and pain-med drip. At long last, the pain disappeared from my body and I started to feel whole again.

"Thank you," I said.

"Sure, man."

The helicopter trip to Kandahar Airfield took about twenty minutes, and for the duration of the flight, the American medic talked with me. He talked with me to keep me focused and calm. We talked mostly about Afghanistan. Later, he gave me a book about the country; inside, he'd written me an inspirational note. He also gave me a patch from his unit. That patch is one of the most treasured items I have from all my time as a soldier.

As soon as we landed at Kandahar, I was rushed to the base hospital. While the doctors prepared for surgery, I was passed a phone. I called my dad.

"Dad, I just want you to know that . . . you're going to hear some stuff about me and get some more details later. But this is just a quick call to let you know that I'm going to be okay."

"What do you mean? Son, what happened?"

"They got me, Dad. The Taliban. But I'm alive and I'm going into surgery. I'm going to get through this. Don't worry."

I hung up and called my mom, but there was no answer. She was probably playing cribbage down at the Legion. I decided not to leave a message. Instead, I called my friend Jeff, the one I'd worried about during the battle for the white schoolhouse and who had been wounded when the A-10 strafed Charles Company.

"Jeff, I'm hit. I'm going into surgery. Go to my mom's house and wait for her. I want you to tell her I called her. I want the first thing you say to her to be 'Jody's okay.' Can you do that for me?" He promised he would.

I hung up. It was time for surgery.

15

CUT OFF

I **WOKE UP** with a doctor looming over me. It took a few moments for the anaesthetics to wear off and for me to remember where I was and what was going on. Then it came back to me in a rush. The mission. The land mine. The pain. The surgery.

The surgeon standing by my bed put it to me bluntly. "I had to cut off both your feet."

"But they told me my left foot would be okay," I said.

"Nope, it was too damaged. I had to take it off as well," he said. Despite his bluntness, I could tell he was upset, probably with himself, for not being able to save my other foot. Half of my brain wanted to yell out, "Hey, go back in there, get my fucking foot and reattach it right now!" But the other half—the more sensible side—knew the surgeon had done his best.

He went on to explain that I had suffered compound fractures of the tibia and fibula on my left leg and the foot was so badly damaged that it was pretty much backwards. "Even if I'd managed to save it, it would have been useless to you."

I imagined a club of meat at the end of my leg.

"I made the decision to amputate mid-calf—on both legs—to try and give you the best chance possible to use prosthetics in the future."

Was I hearing correctly? I thought I'd lost only my feet, but now the surgeon was telling me I'd lost part of my lower legs, too. My initial reaction was to go into denial mode. This won't mean the end of my career in the Canadian Armed Forces. No way. I thought to myself, "There are lots of guys in the Force who use prosthetics." Or so I thought.

I was so convinced of this that the day after my surgery, when all the snipers, including Barry, Kash and Gord, came by the hospital at Kandahar Airfield to see me, I said, "Guys, I'll be fine. I'll go home for a while, do some rehab, get some prosthetic legs, learn how to walk with them and be back on the next mission chasing Taliban."

There was lots of nodding and encouragement, but I'm not sure the guys believed this.

My legs were still all bandaged up, so I couldn't see them. My legs—or what was left of them—were swollen, and the bandages were bloody. I had an external fixator on my left leg. The surgeon had saved as much of the shattered bone as he could and the fixator would hold it in place until, at a later time in Canada, steel plates could be put in. At this point, I was on so many drugs that I didn't feel the pain.

Over the next couple of days, my condition stabilized, until I was strong enough to begin my long journey home to Canada. I flew to Bagram Airfield first, which is the biggest American air base in Afghanistan, located north of Kabul. I had some minor surgery there, and the American doctors made sure that my wounds were free of dirt and debris from the explosion.

A couple of days after that, I flew from Bagram to Kuwait, where we picked up a few more injured soldiers before heading to Ramstein Air Base in Germany. From there it was a short drive to the U.S.

military hospital in Landstuhl. There, I shared a room with another injured Canadian soldier, whose vehicle had been blown up. A Canadian Challenger jet was coming to get him in a couple of days, and I very much wanted to go home with him on that plane. The normal turnaround time at Landstuhl is about two weeks, but my recovery was going well enough that I was given the go-ahead to leave.

On the day of the flight, I was pumped full of blood thinners and pain meds. I was loaded onto the Challenger bound for Toronto. When we touched down, my whole family was there to greet me, as well as my girlfriend. The doors of the jet opened. I was on a stretcher, and as I looked down I saw my brother. "Hey, you're wearing my favourite hat!" I said, which made everyone laugh. Once I was off the plane, everyone wanted to say hi and seemed really happy. I remember soldiers there as well, and it was nice to see some troops in uniform. As I was wheeled away, I gave everyone a big thumbs-up.

They wheeled me on a gurney over to an ambulance, which would take me to intensive care at Sunnybrook hospital. But on the way to the ambulance, one of the medical personnel—she was actually a captain in the Armed Forces—leaned over to me and whispered, "Just so you know, we don't have any idea what we're doing."

"Okay," I said, thinking, "What the fuck does that mean?" It was a very telling comment, one that set the tone for the administrative side of my recovery in the months ahead.

The captain was right. It had been a long time—forty or fifty years—since the Canadian military health care system had had to deal with wounded soldiers coming home from combat. Historically, our military simply hadn't played an active combat role. Our system knew what to do with soldiers coming back in body bags; it also knew how to treat small injuries. But for anything in between—requiring months of rehab and recovery—it was foreign territory.

Once I was checked into the ICU at Sunnybrook, I found out one of the nurses on my floor was Kash's sister. Talk about a small world— I was on the same floor as the sister of one of the key guys in my sniper unit in Afghanistan. I assumed that this would mean I would get some extra-special attention, but as it turned out, I wasn't ever under the care of Kash's sister.

I had received excellent personalized care in Afghanistan and Germany, but I now had to adjust to a whole new system that was entirely different. The staff at the hospital seemed overworked at night, and there were times when my urine bag was overflowing. My girlfriend and my mom (along with anyone else who visited) became my unofficial nursemaids, a job that no one had signed up for. It was a stressful time, for them and for me. My girlfriend at one point got into an argument with one of the nurses, who seriously lacked bedside manner, and this became yet another source of stress for all of us.

One night, my pain medication stopped working after all my family had gone home. I could self-administer the morphine drip by pushing a button at certain intervals, which would release the medication through IV. But on this night, the morphine just wasn't working, and I was in intense pain. It felt like dogs were gnawing on the broken ends of my legs. I pushed the call button on the side of my bed to have my nurse come by and check out the problem. A good thirty or forty-five minutes went by and she still hadn't come by to see me. I was in agony.

Finally, the nurse arrived.

"I haven't been in this much pain since the explosion," I told her. "Can you please call a doctor? Something is wrong."

"Sure," the nurse said. "There's an anesthesiologist on call."

But another two hours went by and nobody came to check on me. At this point, I was in more pain than I have ever been in in my life. In the dead of the night, I had no escape. Even thinking about it now, I'm overwhelmed by the memory of that pain. At the time, I broke down completely. I was crying, the tears streaming down my face. My hand was gripped around the call button, which I pressed over and over again, but still, nobody came.

Eventually, the nurse came back to my room.

"Nurse! I can't take it. Is the doctor coming?"

"It's been a busy night. I'm sorry, but he can't come to see you."

"The pain. There's something wrong. The line's cut off. I'm not getting any pain meds. I swear there's something wrong."

She went to the IV and checked the settings and the line. "I don't see any problems. Just press your button when you need it."

I writhed in pain for the entire night, with no relief. The next morning, a new nurse was assigned to me after shift change. She was a sweet woman who had always gone out of her way to make sure I was comfortable. I was so happy to see that woman's face.

"Thank god you're here!" I said.

"Jody, what's wrong? You look terrible."

"I didn't sleep. I'm in terrible pain. Please, you've got to help me. The pain meds stopped working last night."

The nurse walked over to the IV machine and pushed a couple of buttons. "Okay, Jody. Try pressing your morphine button now."

I pressed it. Within seconds, the pain disappeared.

"Holy shit. What did you do?"

Later, I found out that on that night my morphine drip had only been dispensing one tenth of my usual dosage, and at twice the normal interval.

•

One day during the next two weeks, while a nurse changed my bandages, I got a look at the stumps of my legs. They were covered in stitches and staples and still pretty swollen. I felt embarrassed looking at them. I was always used to being one of the tallest guys in the room, and now I couldn't even stand up. A funny thing about your mind when you lose your feet is that your brain doesn't always remember the loss. There were nights when I'd need to go to the bathroom, and up I'd get, forgetting completely about my accident until I abruptly realized that I didn't have feet to swing off the bed and plant on the floor.

In the daytime, though, I never forgot what had happened. I made an effort to keep moving and to get out of bed on my own.

About ten days into my stay, a nurse came to talk to me. "Jody, we noticed that you urinate, but we're a little concerned that you're not doing much else."

"What do you mean? I go every day," I responded.

"That's impossible," the nurse said. "You've never asked for a bed-pan for that."

"Correct. I get to the bathroom on my own."

"What! How? You never ask for help."

"Because I don't need anyone's help with that," I said.

The nurse was so taken aback that she asked me to demonstrate. Not only that, she called five or six of her colleagues to watch.

"I need a bit of room here," I said. "I'm not used to such a big crowd for this."

They stood back. As soon as I started to pull myself off the bed, one of the nurses came running forward to assist me.

"Just back off," I said. "Because if I land on you, you're going to be the one in this hospital bed."

I shifted to my wheelchair, rolled to the bathroom, and even let the group watch as I transported myself onto the toilet. They watched in amazement.

"Ta-da!" I said as I sat down.

"I can't believe you just did that," one of them said.

"I guess we're not used to dealing with soldiers," another one commented. That was true: they *weren't* used to dealing with soldiers, who generally had a high fitness level, good upper-body strength and an ability to work around difficulties, especially physical ones.

I had been at Sunnybrook for only two weeks when I was transferred to St. John's Rehab, a centre affiliated with the hospital. The nice thing about St. John's was that I could now work towards the goal of walking again. I got my first set of prosthetics in March. One of the first things I asked about them was "Can I carry sixty-five pounds' worth of gear over thirteen kilometres on these?" I was thinking about the army's Battle Fitness Test. "So, will I be able to do that in about a year?"

The prosthetist hesitated. Then he said, "Well . . . we'll definitely have to see." I'm not sure the prosthetist had ever been asked that question before.

From that point on, I made it my mission to learn to walk again. I treated rehab like a military course. When the military wants a soldier to learn something, they send him on a course. So that's the approach I took with my rehab. If you can imagine using stilts, that's probably what using prosthetics feels like. My centre of gravity was completely off, and it was weird that I couldn't feel where my feet used to touch the ground. At first, it was very hard to move. I used parallel bars to support my weight, moving from one end of the bars to the other. This was a major deal, something I'd been working towards for a while. My mom was there, alongside the physiotherapist and the prosthetist. By the time I made it to the other end, Mom was crying and the physiotherapist was crying and the prosthetist was crying, and so was I. The best thing about the first day: peeing standing up—something I hadn't done since before the accident.

From that day on, I never looked back. I grew comfortable with the prosthetic feet. Around that time, I got a letter from some kids at Kennedy Public School in Scarborough. They wanted me to visit and talk about superheroes. I decided that I would leave my cane behind and walk into the library without it, which was the first time I'd done that in public. The kids were all seated quietly and clapped when I arrived. They'd set up a stool for me at the front. I sat down, told them a bit about me and what I'd done in Afghanistan. They asked lots of great questions that I was happy to answer. Overall, it was a great day.

A while later, I got some very good news. A few months earlier, while I was still on tour in Afghanistan, I had fallen in love with a bike that I saw on the cover of *Motorcycle Mojo* magazine. I actually emailed the magazine guys asking how I could get my hands on one of those bikes. But after the accident, I had to send a follow-up email telling them that my situation had changed. I wrote, "I lost both my feet and part of my legs overseas. By any chance, has anybody built a thumb-shift motorcycle? LOL." I assumed that was the end of it.

A few weeks later, my brother, Cory, made up an excuse for us to drive up to Barrie, Ontario. When we got there, we pulled into the Harley dealership.

"What are we doing here?" I asked.

"Oh, nothing much," Cory said.

When we got out of the car, the dealership unveiled a custom-made Harley for me—complete with a thumb-shift. The *Motorcycle Mojo* magazine editors had called the Harley owners in Barrie, and the Harley guys were inspired by my story. They decided I deserved the bike of my dreams. I couldn't believe my eyes. I was absolutely shocked and moved to tears. Just when I thought my dream of riding a motorcycle was over, these guys kept my dream alive. I'll always be grateful to them for that.

By this point, I'd recovered enough to be transferred to ambulatory care. I went to the facility for two or three hours each day for rehab sessions and consultation. We now started to talk about where I might live and transitioning me to a short-term accessible apartment in Toronto. I'd sold my house in Chalk River by then and needed to get set up with a new home. The admin person from the Armed Forces offered three apartments in the area, but none of them were going to work for me. They were either not in the right location for me or they weren't accessible. I could live in military housing in Oakville, but the daily commute to St. John's would have been too long. I gave up on the so-called mobility-friendly options I was being offered and decided to search for myself. I fired up my laptop and punched in "Toronto apartments for rent."

I found a place that was only a few blocks from the rehab centre. I went to the apartment, and sure enough, the doorways were wide enough and the bathroom would do, though it wasn't exactly spacious. I took the place. Yet again, it was obvious that the military system just couldn't quite cope with my needs. Sure, I was offered help with all sorts of things, from rehab to finding a home, but no one truly understood the needs that are particular to a returning soldier. And neither did I.

Once this became clear to me, I started talking to Armed Forces people about ways in which we could improve things for our wounded troops, ways to cut through the red tape and help injured soldiers get what they required during their time of recovery. I talked about wait times and why faster was critical for wounded guys returning from their tours of duty. Sometimes, by the time I was at the top of the list for a service I'd requested, I was past needing it.

My suggestions seemed to get attention, because one day I got called into the Armed Forces base in Toronto to talk about my situation. It didn't quite go the way I'd expected. It was suggested that there might have been complaints that I was being uncooperative and unresponsive.

Unresponsive? I couldn't believe what I was hearing. "I have a cellphone, an email address, a home phone number and I'm on Facebook. I have no missed calls or emails, so what on earth are you talking about?"

I never got an answer to that question. Maybe it was just easier to consider me a problem than deal with the much bigger institutional challenge of how to best assist a wounded soldier. In this area, the American system is more advanced, because they have been dealing with wounded soldiers returning home for a long, long time. To this day, I advocate for adopting best practices from their system so that wounded veterans and their families can be relieved of at least some of the needless stress and focus more energy on recovery.

At one point, the Forces sent me to the Center for the Intrepid, in San Antonio, which at the time was one of the top rehab facilities in the world for soldiers dealing with amputations and other severe injuries. We didn't (and still don't) have anything like this in Canada, so I was sent with another soldier and two Canadian Armed Forces physiotherapists to see what we could learn. The Center is a massive, sprawling complex with everything you could possibly need under one roof: hospital, rehab facility, prosthetic equipment adjustments and living quarters. This facility has cutting-edge technology, both proven and experimental, with some amazing gadgets and devices to assist in the rehabilitation process for someone who is trying to recover from losing both legs.

A virtual-reality dome allows amputees to walk on a treadmill that simulates different terrains, almost like the holodeck in *Star Trek: The Next Generation*. There are exercises where soldiers sit in a boat and lean from side to side to steer through water, building upper-body muscles and practising weight shifts from one side to the other. And just to make sure all of these simulations are safe, soldiers are hooked into a protective harness.

I was completely blown away by these methods of rehabilitation. Most of my rehab had been accomplished on a simple set of parallel bars. I sure didn't have technological gadgets to help me through. I shared my excitement with the two Canadian Forces physiotherapists on the trip.

"That place is amazing!" I said. "It's exactly what someone dealing with amputation needs to recover."

"Pffft. We don't need these toys for rehab," I was told, much to my shock and disappointment.

"These aren't toys to me, they're fucking tools," I said. I let them have a piece of my mind, and by the end of my rant, they got the point. This exchange taught me that a lot of physiotherapists were used to working with soldiers who had small issues—sprains, tennis elbow, pulled muscles. Many had little exposure to veterans facing severe injuries and amputations. Those who'd never had that experience found it hard to justify spending millions of dollars—which of course we didn't have at our disposal—on "fancy gadgets and toys." The question I had was this: if our veterans aren't worth it, who is?

The toughest thing for me, beyond dealing with my own mobility and injury issues, was navigating through a system unprepared for what I needed most. I didn't have a great peer support group around me from the military, either. I was suddenly cut off from this professional family that I'd always turned to for support. In hindsight, I should probably have chosen to do rehab in Ottawa instead of Toronto, because I would have been closer to my home base in Petawawa. There, I would have retained a connection with the gang from 1 RCR. I needed them at that time, through rehab and recovery. It would have been great to have them come by every day and see how I was. One of the recommendations I had for the Armed Forces after my experience was that wounded soldiers should always be at hospitals close to their home base, and that they should be grouped together so they could assist each other throughout recovery. This way, they wouldn't lose touch with their teams and would have the benefit of the support from their military family.

One aspect of support I did receive from the military was ongoing therapy. After my incident, I was referred to a psychologist, who helped me get a handle on a lot of the things that were bothering me. Of course I needed emotional support for the difficulties involved in transitioning to life without two feet. But ironically, one of the biggest emotional problems I had to deal with was the anger I felt towards a medical system that didn't seem able to respond appropriately to my needs. I knew this anger wasn't healthy or productive, and the psychological help allowed me to work on redirecting those sentiments into something more productive.

For the most part, snipers are not prone to suffering from post-traumatic stress disorder, or PTSD, probably because we have a better ability to emotionally detach ourselves on the battlefield and look at war as a job. But even as I improved and started to find my footing—literally and figuratively—I started to wonder if all of my experiences were leading me down the dangerous road of PTSD. In my case, I do think I was dealing with a little bit of it because I had both my feet blown off in Afghanistan. There were so many adjustments I had to make, and there was no manual on how to do anything. I'd put on a whole lot of weight because I couldn't exercise the way I did before my accident. And Dairy Queen is delicious when you're depressed. So in conjunction with the therapy sessions, I also started taking an antidepressant to help control my moods.

And then there was the other kind of pain—the physical kind. I was still using painkillers to help dull the pain that was there each and every day. I needed that relief so badly. But in the end, that, too, caused me tremendous suffering, and I turned into something I never thought I would be—an addict.

16

SOLDIER ON

I WANTED TO walk. I wanted to walk so badly. And I needed to walk, too. But during my time at rehab, I was in incredible pain, not just in my legs but in all the lower part of my body. When I was released from the hospital and became a day patient, I was so relieved. I was happy to be moving on to the next stage in the process. I was put on a med to help with the pain, 200 milligrams, three times per day. I didn't know then that this was a pretty high dosage.

One day at St. John's Rehab, I was watching a TV show called *Intervention*, which follows drug addicts and tells their stories, including the struggles of their family. One segment featured a kid who was raging mad. His family and friends were pleading for him to get off his drugs. The drug he was on wasn't heroine or crack. It was OxyContin.

That triggered something, because the name seemed familiar. This was well before OxyContin had the widely known reputation it has now, way before anyone referred to it as "hillbilly heroin." I grabbed my prescription bottle, and sure enough, the label said OxyContin. So I was on the same drug as that highly addicted kid? I certainly didn't want to become dependent on a substance with the potential to turn people into lunatics.

After doing a Google search on the effects of OxyContin, I contacted my doctor right away and asked to be weaned off this painkiller. Over the next few years, my dosage was lowered to 10 or 20 milligrams day, but it was a slow process.

That day I'd grabbed my bottle and realized I was taking OxyContin, I'd noticed a warning on the bottle not to chew the pills. And here's the proof that maybe the slippery slide had already begun, because instead of heeding the warning, I wondered, "What would happen if I chewed one of these things?" And then I tried it. I chewed my next dose. In no time flat I was as high as a kite and feeling pretty good. I had enough willpower not to do that again, but I slowly started feeling the addictive pull overtaking me even while I feared that very consequence. In no time, I was taking more of the drug than I was supposed to in order to relieve my psychological and physical pain.

I had a prescription refill for every thirty days—on the dot, not earlier, no exceptions. But my pills didn't last that long because I was taking more than my dosage. When I saw the doctor at the base to renew my prescription, he asked me how I had gone through my previous batch so quickly. "I'm just in so much pain, I guess I needed a few extra last month," I told him.

I could tell this doctor was conflicted. On the one hand, he was seeing the clear signs of addiction. On the other, sitting across from him was a soldier who'd recently lost both his feet in an explosion.

In the end, he renewed my prescription, but I knew he would be monitoring me a lot closer from then on. My dosage was now down to 30 to 50 milligrams per day, a lot lower than when I first started using the drug, but I was still burning through them quickly.

I started to concoct stories to secure more pills. I showed up at my doctor's office and told him, "It says right here on the bottle that if you ever spill these pills, you should throw them out immediately. So that's what I did. I spilled them," I said, lying to the man's face.

The addiction worsened, and I started crushing the pills into a powder and snorting it to get a better high. It wasn't like in the movies where someone snorts a line of coke and goes into a fantasy world. This was more like a mellow, gradual high that gave me some relief from the depression I was feeling. I was starting to have doubts about whether I'd return to life as a soldier, and my fears were haunting me. I worried about my future: if I wasn't a soldier, who was I? I had no answer to that question, and again, the thought was disconcerting. Those pills gave me relief from my stress and mental pain, if only for a little while. But as soon as they wore off, my demons would return.

By late 2007, I'd moved back to Petawawa and Chalk River. I had also broken up with my girlfriend. The break-up rate among wounded vets is very high. I think that my returning injured not only changed my life but changed hers, too. And it put a lot of strain on our relationship. At the height of an intense argument between us, she said, "Good luck trying to find anybody else who wants to be with you." I don't blame her for thinking that. I don't blame her for anything, actually. But at the time, the comment stung, because a part of me worried she was right. What if nobody wanted to be with a guy who'd lost both his feet and didn't know where he was headed now? What if I was so damaged—mentally, emotionally and physically—that I offered no value to anyone anymore?

•

Fortunately for me, I did find a woman who was willing to accept me for who I was and with all of the problems that I was facing. I was spending a lot of time on the base in Petawawa and I kept running into people who'd been part of my rescue operation back in Afghanistan and were now back home. It was always great seeing them. But the one person I hadn't run into was Alannah, the medic who was my primary caregiver during my initial transport away from the incident. I really wanted to thank her in person and say hello, but I hadn't seen her anywhere around the base.

One night, I was at a bar when this beautiful blonde floated in. A couple of seconds later, I realized it was Alannah. As she walked past me, I reached out and grabbed her wrist. She immediately cocked her right arm back like she was ready to throw a punch. But once she realized it was me, she unclenched her fist and gave me a big hug. "Holy shit, Jody! How are you?"

We chatted for a few minutes and I told her that I had broken up with my girlfriend and was living by myself. "Also," I said, "I have a brand-new puppy named Charlie." Charlie was a present from a breeder. When I went to pick him up from Mount St. Louis Labradors and gave the breeder the negotiated fee, he said, "Did you know this litter was born on Canada Day? Keep your money. This is my way of thanking you for your service."

"I have a dog, too," Alannah said. "You should bring your puppy to my place." She went on to say that she was having some people over that weekend for a barbecue and invited me to come and hang out. I got her address and was looking forward to it. When I arrived at her place, I was surprised to find it jam-packed with her medic colleagues. As soon as I walked through the front door, they leapt into action to help me out. One of them made me a sandwich, while somebody else set me up in front of the TV with the remote control. I felt like I was the guest of honour. That's what happens when you are with a bunch of medics—they all want to help you out.

I didn't even mind that there were so many people around because neither Alannah nor I was ready to jump into a relationship right away. But there was definitely chemistry. We started hanging out a lot after that. It was less about romance and more about being with someone who had a common experience. After all, she was one of the last people to see me on the ground in Afghanistan. She knew exactly what I'd been through because she'd been there through all of it herself. And even though she hadn't suffered the kind of physical injury I had, she'd seen enough as a medic in Afghanistan to understand some of the psychological issues I was facing. And she, too, was dealing with readjusting to life after Afghanistan. The two of us found a common bond in that, and we helped each other through some of the recovery stages.

Alannah was invaluable to my recovery during those first few months back in Petawawa. Slowly, our deep friendship evolved and I spent a lot more time at her house. She babied me and fed me and generally made me feel better. Over time, our friendship morphed into romance.

At the same time, I was determined to get back to work in the army. I set a target return date of January 10, 2008, so that I would be able to return back less than a year after I was wounded. I couldn't wait to march with my fellow soldiers, in full uniform, on my own two new prosthetic feet. On the day of my return, Barry picked me up. We were going to head over to morning parade together, but I was running a little bit late.

I had encountered an unforeseen problem. It had been almost a year since I had put on my uniform, and when I did, I found it didn't quite fit. I had been a size 34 waist—or smaller—for as long as I could remember, but now I struggled to do up the button on my pants. I tried putting my belt on to keep the pants up, but I couldn't even do up the first notch.

"Look at you. You've turned into a fat fuck!" Barry said, laughing. I was howling as well. I knew he meant no harm, and it was great to find humour in the moment. Besides, nothing was going to get me down on that day. I did up my pants as well as I could, arranging my combat blouse to hang over the front and hide the disaster underneath. I didn't have full strength back in my legs, so I couldn't wear my standard-issue military boots. They were still too heavy. Instead, I walked in the parade wearing a pair of blue running shoes. I was breaking the rules again, but for once, nobody seemed to care. It felt great to be back in uniform with my fellow soldiers.

•

Pieces of my life were starting to fall into place. There was big news on the home front: Alannah was pregnant. And at the base, my back-to-work job was to coach the rifle team for the Canadian Forces Small Arms Competition. I had participated in the same competition in 2002. It was a great group, with some keen privates who didn't have enough experience to act like they knew best, and a few junior corporals as well. We trained all summer long, and at the end of the summer, I told my guys the one event I really wanted them to win was the Soldier's Cup. At this event, soldiers march with full combat load for a certain distance, then shoot, then march again. It's the one event that tries to test battlefield skills, and I was sure my guys had a fighting chance. The day before the competition, Alannah went into labour, which meant my boys had to compete alone. Our daughter, Aylah, was born September 17, 2008. While I was still at the hospital, our newborn in my arms, I got a text from the boys: "We won the Soldier's Cup!" I had two things to be very proud of.

Shortly after that, I was approached by the chief of military personnel in Ottawa about a posting there to help establish a Directorate of Casualty Support Management. My role would be to represent the wounded in developing policy. Also, as part of my new role, I would work at Soldier On, the new program for injured soldiers aimed at helping them deal with their injuries and illnesses. I became an advocate for the cause, doing media interviews to bring awareness to

the problems we were confronting. I was proud to play a part in positive change, but I was extremely frustrated by the lack of proactive
problem-solving and the often inflexible mindset I encountered once
I started working in Ottawa.

For example, my cubicle was only about ten metres away from those
working on my case file, but for whatever reason, I was not consulted
about my issues or approached with inquiries about what I needed.
Maybe that's because people felt it would be crossing some sort of line
from professional to personal, but it seemed mind-boggling to me
that I was sitting right there and my experience, opinions and guid-
ance weren't being regularly sought.

It became clear that life as a paper-pusher wasn't for me. I was determined to get back to Afghanistan on an active tour of duty. The
Americans had a few amputees in active duty. Why couldn't I do the
same in Canada? I saw a posting for a door gunner on a helicopter, a
perfect role for me. I wouldn't have to walk anywhere, and my skill set
as a sniper would be an ideal match. The only barrier was simple to
overcome—I'd need to get from my bunk to the chopper.

The chief of the defence staff at the time, Walter Natynczyk, visited
me at the Soldier On office. "So, what's next for you, Jody?" he asked.
"What's your plan?"

This was my break, so I took the opening. "I want to be a door gunner on a chopper in Afghanistan," I responded.

"Good enough for me," he said. Natynczyk walked to the other end
of the building, air force headquarters, and told them he would really
appreciate if Master Corporal Mitic could have a spot on one of their
helicopters for the next tour. I was thrilled. I had the blessing and support of the man at the top.

But the ultimate decision belonged to the tour commander. And
he came back with the edict that if I wanted to be deployed overseas
again, I had to retake the Battle Fitness Test and the Personal Weapon

Test, standard things for all soldiers before they go on tour. "Fair enough," I thought to myself. "I'll prove that I'm physically capable of doing the job."

The Personal Weapon Test required sprinting in between shooting sessions, and at that point, I still hadn't mastered the art of running on prosthetic feet. The Battle Fitness Test included a 13 kilometre hike to be completed in under two and a half hours while carrying a heavy rucksack. Both these tests would be daunting, but if I committed myself and grinded it out, I felt I could do it.

But then I needed to complete what was called the EXPRES test before even attempting the Battle Fitness Test. It involved a series of quick wind sprints, or rushes, at 20 metre intervals—sprint, turn and sprint back. My prosthetic feet made it virtually impossible for me to stop on a dime, so wind sprints were out of the question. I decided I needed a bit more recovery time to get my skills up to par.

A few months later, my co-worker Andrew at Soldier On, who was a long-distance runner, suggested I try the Army Run half-marathon. Andrew agreed to help train me for the race. He connected me with Phil March, a long-distance running expert and great trainer. Together, they came up with a plan to get me into shape. Maybe I could impress the chain of command and convince them I had what it took to go back overseas.

I did the 21.2 kilometre half-marathon run in just about three and a half hours. I talked to General Leslie, chief of the land staff, after I crossed the finish line. "See? I've got what it takes. I want to be the gunner on that helicopter." It was very shortly thereafter that I realized that a run on flat terrain with water stations and bathrooms dotting the route and crowds cheering me on the whole way wasn't exactly the same as a tour in Afghanistan. Even with all that, the half-marathon still kicked my ass. Here I was wanting to go back to a war zone, but in truth, my being there would more than likely have been a liability. Beyond that, I'd be putting so much strain on my body that it would take a permanent toll. I had to ask myself: did I want to be in a wheelchair at fifty-five because I had worn out my body?

•

It was after that half-marathon that I reluctantly decided to say goodbye to my life as a soldier. I tell people that Jody the soldier was wounded in January of 2007, but it took him about two years to die. At some point, I just had to accept that the big green machine would be fine without me. The war in Afghanistan would continue. Kash, Barry and Gord would carry on in their sniper roles.

Of course, this wasn't an easy decision for me, and I was filled with rage and anger. And again, I started using OxyContin as a relief from the pain of loss. It became a problem yet again, but I deluded myself into believing I had it under my control. I didn't want to alert my colleagues—or Alannah—to the struggle I was having with an addiction. I felt I was hiding the problem fairly well, although my new doctor in Ottawa was getting more and more suspicious about my actions.

I went from monthly prescriptions to twice-a-month prescriptions, which meant my doctor could keep a closer eye on me. I'd go through two weeks' worth of pills in about five days. "Doctor, I need some more pills," I'd say, arriving at his office earlier than expected. He started issuing me pills on a weekly basis. It got to a point where I was burning through them faster than he could prescribe them.

Finally, one day he said, "You're going to have to come in each day for your dose."

Every day? Who did he think I was? Of course, this was the addiction talking, and at the time I didn't want to face the fact that I was reaching a dangerous tipping point. Because I could no longer feed my addiction through prescriptions, I turned to a new source: I secured black-market Percocet and began taking that to replicate my OxyContin high.

One day, I was reading a *Reader's Digest* article about how this one OxyContin addict would heat up the drug into a liquid form and then inject himself to get a high. He knew it was time to quit when his daughter caught him about to shoot up.

My first thought wasn't "That is awful." It was "Hmm. I didn't know you could inject it." My next thought was "Why did I fucking think that?" And that thought scared me enough to take action. I asked for help from the army. I wanted to take a three-day "spin dry" course that was meant to help veterans with their addictions, but I didn't receive much of an enthusiastic response to my wanting to go that route. "I don't know if we're at that point yet," the doctor said. So I took matters into my own hands.

To celebrate Father's Day in 2011, Alannah and Aylah and I had lunch at Boston Pizza. At one point I went into the bathroom and took my last pill. I decided it was time to man up. "That's it. Time to suck it up," I told myself in the mirror.

I returned to the table and said to Alannah, "I'm quitting. I'm not taking any more OxyContin. I just took my last pill." I knew the next three nights were going to be rough, and I warned Alannah how bad it would be. I don't think she knew just how addicted I was to the painkillers. She knew only that I would have issues if I didn't get my pills on time. I'd masked my addiction pretty well, considering we were living under the same roof and were raising a young daughter together.

Those three days were absolute horror. I slept on our couch every night so I could be by myself. I find it almost impossible to describe what withdrawal felt like and how strongly my body called out for more drugs. The first night, I was in excruciating pain. It felt like my body had ants crawling all over it and that my feet had been blown off again. There was a big hole in my chest and I felt anxious. I couldn't fall asleep and I was constantly grinding the stumps of my legs against the leather couch to get some relief from the pain I felt there. I was rubbing my skin raw and only making things worse. I was bawling like a little baby and couldn't stop. Honestly, quitting OxyContin was harder and more painful than getting blown up in Afghanistan.

I stumbled over to the kitchen and had sugary cereal to spike my system. It helped temporarily; then I was back to the agony. I was at my worst the next morning when Aylah, who was three years old at the time, came downstairs. My beautiful little girl sat on the couch with me and asked if we could watch cartoons together.

"Of course we can," I said. She settled in next to me on the couch. I knew then that I had a new duty. I had to keep it together for my daughter. And I did. She gave me the strength and focus I needed to get through those early hours. She never knew the favour she did for me that day.

The days that followed were still hellish, but nothing like that first one. And after those three days, things got better. I was drained of energy for a while. The next three months I was like a new computer booting up. I was reloading my operating system in the hopes of being able to function normally. And with time, I wasn't addicted to OxyContin anymore.

That didn't mean that life suddenly got rosier. It didn't. I felt lethargic and had a hard time motivating myself. I still had big questions I needed to answer in order to move forward: what was I going to do with my life now? What did I actually want, and what was possible? And could I really put my military past behind me and pursue something else that would make me feel fulfilled?

But it was time to stop asking questions. It was time to find some answers.

EPILOGUE

ON MY OWN TWO FEET

WHEN I was eleven years old and the Olympic torch was to be carried through Calgary, I really wanted to carry it. I filled out a card in *Reader's Digest* hoping to be the lucky winner of the opportunity to carry that torch. I didn't get the chance to fulfill that childhood dream until 2010, when I was asked to carry the Olympic torch in Ottawa. I felt incredibly proud to be representing my country and carrying that symbol on one little part of its journey to Vancouver. On the day of the run, I was getting ready when a stranger came over to speak to me. We went on talking for a while and she told me that she'd heard the story of my injuries in Afghanistan and that she'd been inspired by my determination to walk and even run again. She said, "I lost a hundred pounds because of you." She went on to explain that because I was able to get over adversity, she knew she could. And she succeeded.

As my story became more public, I was stopped more often by people who had drawn inspiration from my experiences. And each time they told me their stories, I found myself getting stronger. It made me realize that people were looking at me to be an example. And since that was the case, I knew I had to be the best role model possible.

In 2013, I auditioned for *The Amazing Race Canada* with my brother, Cory. The producers called us back and wanted us on the show. I was excited because I had a message to deliver to a wider audience than just soldiers. When viewers saw an ex-soldier who had lost both of his legs below the knees doing all sorts of crazy activities, they might ask themselves, "What's my excuse for not getting active?" I wanted all Canadians to know that they could and should stay physically active and that they, too, could challenge themselves to the limit. At the end of the season, Cory and I placed second overall out of nine teams and narrowly missed being the champions. But more important, we demonstrated that as competitors we would never quit.

I retired from the military in June of 2014. This may sound like a terrible thing to say, but there is a part of me that will always be envious of soldiers who die on the battlefield. They left this earth doing what they loved, and there is something extremely admirable about dying in that manner. Veterans with injuries are left largely on their own and have to figure out a way to move on and to reinvent themselves. For true soldiers, that is one of the most difficult experiences. A lot of professional athletes will tell you they miss two things when they retire—the competition on the field and the camaraderie with teammates in the locker room. It's the exact same thing for soldiers after we leave the Armed Forces. To this day, I miss the adrenaline rush of the battlefield. I miss being in the barracks with my fellow soldiers. When I see soldiers on parade, I still get chills down my spine because I loved it so much.

After my injury, I was told I could remuster to another military trade, but that would have meant doing a desk job. Being in combat was the whole reason I was in the army, so I couldn't imagine taking on a job outside of the infantry. Also, any position I took would have been a demotion, which felt to me a bit like a punishment for having been wounded. I don't believe that was the intention at all, but it was an unfortunate side effect.

The good news is that leaving the army made room in me for building a strong family and learning to identify with my roles as a father and husband. My second daughter, Kierah, was born in 2011, so I am now the proud father of two lovely girls. My girls ground me and have given me a fresh perspective on life. I always joke that I'm going to force my girls to become soldiers for at least a couple of years so they can get a taste of the army life. While they may be just a tad young for that right now, the real point I'm making is that the Armed Forces make you a more humble person and a better role model for those around you.

My time on *The Amazing Race Canada* made me better known to Canadians, many of whom urged me to consider politics once the show was over. I gave that some thought, and in the end, I decided that my mission has always been to serve my country. A life in politics wasn't my first career choice, but it would offer me a chance to continue to serve my community. In October 2014, I was elected city councillor for Innes Ward in Ottawa, representing over forty thousand constituents. I now have another opportunity to influence the world around me—although this time it's from inside city hall. When I look out my office window, I stare directly at National Defence headquarters. It's a constant reminder that the Armed Forces will always be a part of who I am.

I want to make sure that veterans are involved in politics and that veterans' issues are at the forefront of our political discourse and policy. I take my advocacy very seriously, and I will always devote extra time and energy to issues concerning veterans. Royals have an open invitation to sleep on my couch. Every other member of the military has an open invitation to call or visit my office. I'm part of veterans' networking groups because I believe that no one can look after us better than we can ourselves. Only we know what each other has experienced.

When I moved into my office at city hall, one of the first things I did was hang up a poster of Bruce Lee. It says, "The highest art is no art. The highest form is no form." I have never been one to work well inside the box. I like to think beyond it, to be open to new experiences and to other people's points of view. I put that poster on my wall to remind me that nothing stays the same forever, and that change is a positive force. We can all reinvent and reimagine ourselves, no matter what calamity has befallen us.

When I think back to my time in the Armed Forces, I realize that mentality was always with me. I never feared that I would die on the battlefield, because I was more concerned with the mission and the objective. And when I look back at my time in Afghanistan, I'm proud to say that we achieved some of the goals we set out to accomplish. Because of our mission, little girls who were the same age as my daughters are now were able to go to school for the first time in their lives. And when little boys went to school, they weren't being brainwashed into a damaging way of life. As soldiers, we helped people gain access to medical care, we helped them build roads and we improved the quality of life for thousands of people. We can't control what happens in Afghanistan in the next ten or twenty years, but I like to think that we helped establish the groundwork for Afghan citizens to have a better future.

Most of all, I think we re-established national pride in our military. For years, it was frowned upon to even walk out in public wearing a combat uniform. If soldiers wanted to go grocery shopping or stop off at the mall, we were instructed to go home and change into civilian clothing first. Yet our culture has now shifted so that soldiers are celebrated in public.

People often ask if I regret my time in Afghanistan because it cost me two feet and completely changed my life. If you live your life with regrets, then you never move forward. Those six months in Afghanistan before the explosion were some of the best times of my life. I can honestly say as I look back on my life in the military, I wouldn't have changed a thing. If I hadn't stepped on that land mine, I never would have connected with Alannah. I never would have had two beautiful daughters. My mind and body were pushed to the limit after my accident and, ironically, I came out on the other side a better, more complete person. Maybe my life would be easier now if I hadn't lost a part of both legs, but it certainly wouldn't have been any more complete.

When I am in public today, advocating for veterans' rights or simply going about my daily life, people sometimes approach me to say, "Thank you for your service." Those five words mean more to me than anything else.

ACKNOWLEDGEMENTS

To all of my military brothers and sisters who helped me over my twenty-year career: I only have space here to mention a few people specifically, but there are countless others to whom I owe a debt of gratitude—thank you.

Thanks to the Royal Canadian Regiment—*pro patria*.

To General Rick Hillier, for contributing the foreword to this book and for being the right leader at the right time for the Canadian Forces.

To Brigadier-General Omer Lavoie, for being a soldier's soldier on the battlefield and off.

Thanks to all the soldiers of Roto 03-06, 1 RCR battle group, for being there when your country called you.

Thanks to everyone on call sign 6-3, especially Kash, Gord and Barry. There are no words that will be good enough, so I'll just say I love you all.

To my group of personal heroes who were there for me on the morning of January 11, 2007. You know who you are. Thank you for my life.

To Brian Wood, for smoking all my cigars (haha) and for helping negotiate the best deal a guy like me could get. To Ian Mendes for showing up at the right time and helping me put my thoughts to keyboard.

To Kevin Hanson, for taking a chance by publishing me. To my editor, Nita Pronovost, for making sure my story resonated. Thanks, too, to the group behind the scenes—Sarah St. Pierre, Brendan May and Patricia Ocampo, and to my publicist, Rita Silva.

ACKNOWLEDGEMENTS

To Mom, Dad, Katie and Cory—thank you for supporting me at every step. Thanks, too, to my aunts, uncles, cousins and other family members, all of whom have been there whenever I needed. And to Charlie, for being my buddy.

Finally, thanks to Alannah and to my girls, Aylah and Kierah, for supporting me on this adventure and on all of the ones yet to come.

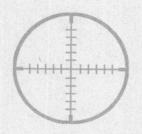

JODY'S GLOSSARY OF MILITARY TERMS

I N the army, we use a lot of terms and expressions that aren't readily understood by most civilians. Our terminology can be very specific and at times fairly colourful. Some of these terms appear throughout the book and some do not. I've included a selection below to let you in on "soldier speak."

Bag drive: a difficult ordeal. E.g., "Our final training exercise was a bag drive."

Boot fuck: to inflict punishment by kicking with one's army boot. E.g., "You pissed me off, so I'm going to boot fuck you," or, figuratively, "We got boot fucked by the enemy."

Barracks: where soldiers set up their digs, also called "the shacks."

Carl Gustav: an awesome recoilless rifle. The Carl Gustav is a good piece of kit (*see also* "Good piece of kit").

Calling in artillery: directing artillery fire onto a desired target via radio.

Cam: short for "camouflage" (*see also* "Stealth").

Combat soldiers: the front line of the army, also thought of as "the pointy end of the spear."

FOBit: a soldier who never leaves the forward operating base (*see also* "Hesco hobbit").

Frag vest: short for "fragmentation vest." The vest is designed to protect the wearer from exploding elements in a grenade, mortar round or artillery round. As a combat soldier, it is entirely advisable to wear gear such as a frag vest and a helmet at all times during a mission, though in Afghanistan I rarely did.

Gear geek: a soldier who always has to have the latest piece of equipment. Gear geeks often get a jacking (*see also* "Jacking") by other soldiers when they pull out their geek gear.

Gerber tool: an army-issued multi-tool that includes implements such as a knife, screwdriver, wire cutter, can opener, ruler, file and saw. The Gerber tool can be used for everything from prepping detonators for plastic explosives to cleaning underneath your fingernails after a long day (*see also* "Good piece of kit").

Ghillie suit: a sniper's personalized camouflage clothing meant to help with blending into any environment. The ghillie suit is a sniper's superhero cape, allowing him to magically disappear in plain sight.

Good go: when soldiers are sent to do a task or job that's cool. E.g., "That mission turned out to be a good go."

Good piece of kit: a piece of equipment that is useful. E.g., "That GPS is a good piece of kit."

G Wagon: a standard armoured vehicle in the Canadian Forces. This vehicle replaced the Iltis that T.J., Beerenfenger and Shorty got blown up in (*see* chapter 10, "Into Afghanistan: Improvise, Adapt, Overcome").

Hesco bastion: a semi-permanent blast wall that protects against explosions or small arms.

Hesco hobbit: someone who never leaves the safety of a Hesco bastion.

Jacking: a reprimand. E.g., "I just got a jacking from the sergeant for being late."

Junk: (1) a piece of army equipment. When a soldier gets a new piece of gear, the first thing he or she does is try to break it. The easier it is to break, the more "junk" it is; the sturdier it is, the less "junk" it is. (2) a bad soldier. E.g., "That soldier is junk."

Over: normally, a radio communication term to signal to the listener that the speaker is done talking. Soldiers will also use the term in normal conversation to signal a rhetorical question. E.g., "What the fuck? Over."

Reconnaissance: military observation to locate an enemy or to gather information. Also known as "recce."

Rope testers: according to retired U.S. Navy Seal Commander Richard Marcinko, the 10 percent of troops who somehow passed all the tests but still have no right being in the army. He quipped that these were the soldiers one should send up a rope to test if it is securely tied, because if it isn't, not much would be lost.

Rucksack: bags that never seem big enough for all of a soldier's gear. Also known as "rucks."

Sacrifice: to volunteer to serve your country, no matter what the personal cost.

Sixth sense: that little tingling sensation at the back of your neck that tells a sniper the enemy is near, even though he can't be seen, smelled or heard.

Soldier: everyman or everywoman. A soldier can be anyone, with any kind of personality, provided that this person can work in a team. This is someone with a level of discipline that is rare in civilian life and common in the military. A soldier fights for the honour of his or her fellow soldiers and for the citizens of his or her nation (*compare with* "Warrior").

Stealth: the result of superior cam and concealment (*see also* "Cam").

Warrior: individual who fights to defend their personal honour, not for the honour of others. Rome, for instance, conquered the world not with warriors but with soldiers (*see also* "Soldier").

ABOUT THE AUTHOR

JODY MITIC is a twenty-year Canadian Armed Forces veteran and sniper-team leader. A sought-after motivational speaker, he is a respected advocate for wounded veterans, people with disabilities and amputees. He founded the Never Quit Foundation and currently sits on the board of directors of Won with One, an organization devoted to helping physically challenged athletes realize their dreams. He currently serves on the Ottawa City Council. Jody lives in Ottawa with his wife, Alannah, and their two daughters, Aylah and Kierah.

🐦 @JODYMITIC

unflinchingbook.ca

Simon & Schuster
Reading Group Guide

UNFLINCHING

JODY MITIC

1. General Rick Hillier says in his foreword that Jody's "perpetual optimism" is invaluable because it can inspire hope and confidence in Canadian soldiers. How do you feel about the Canadian military after reading about Jody's incredible, traumatic journey from start to finish? How would you feel if someone other than Jody had written his story?

2. What do you think initially attracted Jody to the military? What was it about being a soldier that fulfilled him?

3. As a sniper, Jody describes feeling like an outsider, especially in team military operations. What made him feel this way? What does his experience say about the necessary qualifications and personality traits for becoming a sniper?

4. Jody talks about being part of several military operations in the Middle East, such as the first deployment of Canadian peacekeeping troops to Afghanistan, Operation Rocket Man and Operation Medusa. How has your understanding of those operations changed after reading about them from Jody's perspective?

5. After returning home, Jody had to confront the Canadian military's inexperience in rehabilitating disabled soldiers. What do you think could be done to improve the treatment and care of veterans in Canada?

6. Given Jody's decision to go into politics after retiring from the military, what do you think living a life of service means to Jody? Are there skills that Jody learned as a soldier that helped him in his position as an elected representative? What does "service" mean to you? Has your understanding of it changed after reading this book?

7. Jody is up-front about his mistakes, his frustration and his doubts. How does his honesty affect your understanding of his story? Does Jody's matter-of-fact way of talking about his past differ from how you think about your own?

8. One of Jody's signature traits is his unfailing humour, which goes hand-in-hand with his optimism. What purpose does this serve as he recounts his extraordinary trauma? Is humour an essential skill for a high-stress, high-stakes job in the military?

9. *Unflinching* focuses on Jody's extensive training, first for basic, and then for ever more specialized positions, all leading to his role as a sniper. Not only does Jody's completion of this training demonstrate his hardworking nature, it also shows his dedication. What is your passion? What dream would you complete years of training and preparation to achieve?

10. Did you identify with any of Jody's difficulties getting into, and then rising through the ranks of, the Canadian military? If so, which ones and why?